A TREASURY
of
SOUTHERN
BAKING

A Treasury
of
Southern
Baking

Luscious Cakes, Cobblers, Pies, Custards, Muffins, Biscuits, and Breads in the Tradition of the American South

PRUDENCE HILBURN

Photographs by Randall Terry
Illustrations by Clair Moritz

HarperPerennial
A Division of HarperCollins*Publishers*

HarperCollins books may be purchased for educational, business, or sales promotional use. For information, please write: Special Markets Department, HarperCollins Publishers, Inc., 10 East 53rd Street, New York, NY 10022.

FIRST EDITION

Designed by Helene Berinsky

Library of Congress Cataloging-in-Publication Data

Hilburn, Prudence, 1936–
A treasury of southern baking : luscious cakes, cobblers, pies, custards, muffins, biscuits, and breads in the tradition of the American South / by Prudence Hilburn; photographs by Randall Terry.
—1st ed.
p.   cm.
Includes index.
ISBN 0-06-096597-5(pbk.)
1. Baking.   2. Cookery, American — Southern style.   I. Title.
TX765.H55   1993
641.8'15—dc20   92-53401

93 94 95 96 97 DT/RRD 10 9 8 7 6 5 4 3 2 1 (pbk.)

This book is dedicated in love to my husband, Huey;
our daughters, Debra, Twila, and Carol;
and in loving memory of our son, Randy.

Contents

Acknowledgments

I know that I must have the most supportive family in the world. My husband, Huey, knowing how much I love to cook, has always insisted that I get the best training possible. He made arrangements for me to study with James Beard because he knew that had been my desire for many years. When I had the opportunity to travel to the South of France for cooking classes with Simone "Simca" Beck, he was right there with the necessary finances and support. Then I was offered a job at Peter Kump's New York Cooking School and his reaction was "go for it!" He has always encouraged me to follow my dream and, with his help, the dream became a reality.

A big thank-you goes to Peter Kump, who gave me my first job in the food field. Not only was he my boss but he was, and still is, a special friend.

To Barbara Kafka, words cannot express how very much I appreciate her support and her faith in my ability to perform as a food professional. She is not only my mentor, she's also my friend.

I appreciate so very much the many hours my assistant, Mauna Reynolds, spent in my kitchen testing and retesting the recipes. When I needed her, all I had to do was call. Her love of food preparation made working together on this book a true joy.

Randall Terry is responsible for the photographs in the book and I want to thank him for working with me on this project.

I would also like to thank Susan Friedland, my editor, for being so patient with first-time authors. Her expert advice and guidance have helped me to realize that there's more to writing a good book than just gathering favorite recipes.

Introduction

·······•••••••)⊃⊗⊂(••••••••····

It is a pleasure to introduce Prudence Hilburn to you. You will like her and her baking. I suppose all of us who are interested in food hold someplace in our hearts the image of a warm and wonderful gray-haired grandmother who lovingly produces a bounty of baked goods that perfume her kitchen and make children and adults alike happy. Add to that fantasy that she is a Southerner with a long tradition of marvellous biscuits, pies and cakes, someone who is so adept at her craft that she has won innumerable prizes for baking—so many that she has been barred from a number of contests—and you have Prudence. I should also add that, after raising her children, with dedication and the support of a loving and understanding husband, her beloved Huey, she took almost two years to study and work in Europe and New York to learn and absorb as much as she could from a range of cooks and teachers.

What is such a Southern baker? It's a woman who makes biscuits every morning for Huey, who bakes every day as I might make a salad. For Prudence baking is natural and easy, something to share with friends, relatives and readers of her weekly newspaper column. She bakes every day and makes something for every meal.

America has a baking tradition, particularly in the South, that is different from the rest of the world. When Europeans came to America, they came from a world where white flour was restricted to professional bakers and the privileged few. They lived in towns and the town had a bread baker. It was his oven that was used for long-baked dishes. Cakes and pies were special treats. They arrived in a country where when white flour was milled, it was useable by all. They lived on disseminated farms with their own ovens and their own baking. Corn was easier to grow and cornmeal was a cheap, plentiful staple. In the South, the flour was made from warm-weather soft wheat.

It was these realities that shaped the baking repertoire. Soft flour and corn flour don't marry as well with yeast as hard flour, nor do they easily make a starter that can be used from batch to batch of baking. Bread made with hard flour and a starter stays fresh much longer than bread made without them. The upshot was quick breads served hot from the oven and light, elegant cakes, happier without the hard-wheat richness of gluten. The tradition became so entrenched that it was deemed, pejoratively, Northern and lacking in hospitality to serve cold breads. Soft flour also made flakier, more fragile crusts to be the pride of the farm housewife. Not at the beginning, but as the years went on, sugar became available, and, bought, it was a sign of luxury.

Locally grown nuts—pecans and black walnuts—as well as a variety of fruits find their home in Prudence's baking and she uses that ubiquitous Southern pan, the black iron skillet. She shares numerous recipes for cookies, the kind this real grandmother keeps on hand for children as well as those good enough for parties.

It is out of this rich tradition with its love of quick breads (read muffins and biscuits) and handsome cakes with sweet fillings that Prudence comes.

Her gift to you, an extension of Southern hospitality, is this book that makes her recipes and that of her heritage doable by bakers everywhere. She is a home baker aware of the pitfalls and shortages of time that abound in everyone's life. She makes her recipes clear, affordable and sure guides to success. She even includes ways to doctor up things that you buy, like mixes.

The heart of her book is her recipes for Southern favorites, biscuits of several kinds, including the ones she makes hot and fresh every morning for Huey's breakfast. If you would rather have muffins, there are muffins. There are true American layer cakes like the Lady and Lord Baltimore cakes. There are homey inventions, the kind that Prudence makes taste wonderful and inevitably right as well as gala desserts for the end of your very best parties.

Each recipe has a little something special that makes it better, sets it apart. The Fresh Blackberry Cobbler is simple, delicious and uses a sort of biscuit dough crust just the way her mother's did. The Chocolate Bread Pudding cleverly uses chocolate milk instead of plain. The dough for her Apple Dumpling is made with apple juice and the dumplings themselves cook in a rich caramel sauce. There are the pound cakes beloved of the South and the breads from Southern Cornbread to the less-known, but equally traditional Sweet Potato Bread. Bran gives texture and originality to an apple coffeecake and there are dinner rolls. Some of the rolls are good enough to make a tea party on their own, Pineapple Cream Rolls and Cinnamon Rum Rolls.

Reading this book is a special delight for me as it evokes Prudence's voice, gentle and unhurried. I know personally Prudence's warmth, generosity and baking. When she was meeting the food people and learning in New York, she worked with me. I think that once you have read Prudence and used her recipes, you will feel as I do that you have a good friend, and a good friend in the kitchen.

Barbara Kafka

A TREASURY
of
SOUTHERN
BAKING

An Inside Look
AT
Southern Baking

INTRODUCTION

I grew up in a Southern home where the kitchen was the center of activity. I only wish that I could spread the word throughout the cooking world that there is more to Southern cuisine than just "grits and greens and overcooked beans!" This section of our country is blessed with great bakers.

In most Southern homes, there is always something baking in the oven. When I was growing up, the aroma of freshly baked buttermilk biscuits made getting up in the morning a delightful experience. It was important to get to the kitchen while the biscuits were still hot enough to melt the freshly churned butter. The baking of biscuits has been a family tradition for generations and I am the proud owner of my grandmother's large wooden dough bowl, which has the markings of longtime use.

Being the youngest of seven children, I was not allowed to help with the cooking. I remember standing at the end of our large table watching Mother perform her biscuit "magic" and thinking how easy she made it look.

Freshly baked breads sometimes appear on the Southern table three times a day, but there is more to baking than just breads. At our home, no meal is complete without dessert and a simple bowl of fruit will not do—unless it is accompanied by a generous slice of cake or some homemade cookies.

Calories are forgotten when pecan pie, sweet potato cobbler, bread pudding with bourbon sauce, or fresh coconut cake is on the menu.

Too many times when we get in the mood for baking, we pick up a baking book and, much to our disappointment, we find recipes that only a trained pastry chef or an accomplished baker can make. Even when the recipe appears simple, it might call for pans that are not found in most households or ingredients that can't be picked up at the neighborhood market.

This started me thinking. Why not write a baking book for the average homemaker or the amateur weekend pastry chef? After all, these are the kinds of recipes that I enjoy the most and sharing has always been important to me. The best word to describe this type of baking is "homestyle."

Some of the recipes have been passed down from generation to generation and many of them had to be duplicated from memory because my mother seldom used a recipe when she baked. There are even recipes for those who rely on convenience products and are not easily persuaded to bake from scratch. With a little creativity, a dessert "made from a box" can be turned into an elegant but easy creation, one that might even fool the pros!

There are also some quick-and-easy "from scratch" recipes in the Busy Baker section. These recipes can prove very useful to those who work away from home and must budget their time in the kitchen. The Busy Baker recipes will give you quality baked products that are quick and easy.

Baking can be a lot of fun, so grab that apron and head to the kitchen. Enjoy!

A Peek into the Cupboard and Cooler

To fully understand Southern baking, you must first understand some of the ingredients used in most Southern kitchens.

Nowhere in the country is self-rising flour more popular than in the Southern states. This is not just any self-rising flour, but the kind that is milled from soft winter wheat. If you want the old-fashioned, light and fluffy biscuits that are so often associated with Southern baking, this soft flour is a must. This does not mean that you cannot get very good biscuits using other flour, but you will not get the same airy lightness inside and the semicrisp outside that this special soft flour produces.

If self-rising flour is called for in a recipe and all you have is all-purpose flour, you can make your own version of self-rising by adding 1 tablespoon baking powder and 1 teaspoon salt to 2 cups all-purpose flour.

For most of the recipes, any of the nationally marketed all-purpose flours will work fine. In fact, only a few recipes in the book call for self-rising flour. The majority specify all-purpose flour. Bread flour, which is higher in gluten, than all-purpose flour, is used for loaves of white bread and for the yeast dinner rolls. When measuring flour, I use the "stir, scoop, and level" method. After sitting on the shelf for a while, flour will become packed and should be stirred to aerate and lighten it. Failure to do so will often result in too much flour being added to the batter or dough. After stirring the flour, I lightly scoop it into the measuring cup and then level it with the back of a long knife or spatula.

I use only large eggs in all my recipes. For best results, don't substitute small or medium eggs for the large.

Margarine, still referred to by many Southerners as "oleo," has been a popular substitute for butter in the South for as long as I can remember. Yes, even before the cholesterol scare. This is not to say that butter is no longer used; it is. In most of my recipes, I give you the option of using butter or margarine. In order to interchange the two, I suggest that you use a lightly salted butter. If you prefer to use unsalted butter, you might find it necessary to slightly increase the amount of salt in the recipe.

You will also find that solid vegetable shortening is used a lot in Southern baking, even for cakes. When oil is needed, my personal preference is canola oil, but any vegetable oil will give you satisfactory results.

When milk is listed as an ingredient, this means whole milk. It is not unusual to hear a Southerner call it "sweet milk" and I really don't know why. I have substituted 2 percent fat milk in many of the recipes with good results. Buttermilk is often used in Southern baking and lends a special tartness that enhances the flavor in breads and cakes.

The Southerner's "sweet tooth" is often satisfied by sweetened condensed milk in desserts. Whipping cream also finds its place among our high-caloric favorites, but it is not unusual to find Southern bakers using the frozen, non-dairy topping, especially in pies and on top of cakes.

Instead of making the classic buttercream icing, most Southern bakers rely on a more simple version using confectioners' sugar. A love of caramel gives brown sugar a place of importance in the Southern cupboard as well.

There are many kinds of fruit and nut trees in the South so it is not surprising to find many recipes in this book using apples, oranges, pears, peaches, pecans, peanuts, and black walnuts. Strawberries, blackberries, and huckleberries (or blueberries) are plentiful in the South and make an excellent filling for cobblers.

The chocolates used by the average Southern baker are such domestic brands as Bakers, Hershey, and Nestlé. If you have imported chocolate, however, by all means use it.

Southerners love coconut in almost any cake, pie, cookie, and bread. This versatile ingredient can turn a Plain Jane dessert into an elegant-tasting delight. When a recipe calls for coconut, it means the kind that you buy at the supermarket either in cans or plastic bags. If fresh or frozen is to be used, it will be clearly specified.

The Southern trio of spices includes cinnamon, cloves, and nutmeg. Although others are used from time to time, these three are the most preferred. The nutmeg is best when freshly grated.

Some of the important mixes usually found on the Southern shelf are buttermilk baking mix, pie crust mix, cake mix, and muffin mix. All these can be turned into creative desserts and breads.

Southern ingredients can be summarized in two words: simple and basic.

Tools of the Trade

The proper kitchen utensils are as important to a baker as a hammer is to a carpenter. For many years, I thought that all I needed was a portable mixer and a pan or two. However, when I bought a heavy-duty mixer and added to my pan collection, I learned how much easier the job is when you have the right tools.

Personally, I think that the food processor is an indispensable tool of the trade. It not only chops and slices to perfection, but also is excellent for kneading small batches of bread dough. I also use it quite often for quickly mixing cookie dough.

For years, I used the same cookie sheets that had turned dark with age and usage. Then a friend told me about the new insulated cookie sheets. I bought one even though it was expensive and I was skeptical that it would actually be worth the difference. Believe me, it is! Just to prove a point, I made a batch of cookies and baked part of them on my old cookie sheet and another portion on the new insulated one. It was amazing! The cookies were baked at the same temperature and for the same length of time. The ones baked on my old sheet almost burned, while the ones baked on the insulated cookie sheet were ideal.

You will note that most of the cookie recipes in this cookbook will call for lining the baking sheet with aluminum foil. I am assuming that many kitchens are not yet equipped with the new insulated cookie sheets. Of course, if you have one of these super baking sheets, you can omit the aluminum foil.

To the Southern baker, no kitchen is complete without at least one iron skillet. It is definitely the tool of choice for baking corn bread and pineapple upside-down cake. My mother always used a 10-inch iron skillet for baking biscuits.

When I was growing up, the "chimney" pan was very important, especially at Christmastime when Mother was making fruitcakes. This unusual pan is nothing more than what we now call a tube pan. Today's bakers don't wait until the holidays to pull this useful "tool" out of the pantry.

The fancier version of the tube pan, the Bundt pan, became very popular in the 1960s when the Tunnel of Fudge Cake made its appearance on the dessert scene. When Ella Helfrich of Houston, Texas, entered this cake in the Pillsbury Bake-Off, it not only won a prize of $5,000, but also introduced the baking public to the Bundt pan. According to the Pillsbury Company, they had more than 200,000 requests for information about this new pan.

The "sheet cake" pan made an impact on Southern baking, perhaps because it was used to make a cake that was cooked in one large layer and iced in the pan. This quick-and-easy method of baking a cake caught on quickly. Almost every Southern baker added this 9x13x2-inch baking pan to the list of necessary utensils.

Of course, no kitchen tool cabinet is complete without a set of 8- or 9-inch cake pans, 9-inch pie pans, muffin tins (both the standard size and the miniature ones), and the popular loaf pan.

Equipped with the right tools and a cookbook full of recipes that delight the palate, you are now ready to bake!

Cakes

On the list of favorite Southern desserts, cakes are at the top. Christmas was a special time for cakes when I was growing up because they were not an everyday item.

Mother didn't bake just one or two cakes during the holidays. When time came for dessert after our Christmas meal, we always found a dessert table loaded with at least 10 cakes. Among those were the Lane cake, a chocolate cake, Lady Baltimore cake, hickory nut cake, the traditional fresh coconut cake, Granny's special coconut cake, fruitcake, icebox fruitcake, and date pecan cake.

There are also some newly developed cakes such as velvet fudge cake, strawberry ribbon cake, and chocolate-covered cherry cake that are sure to become family favorites.

If you want to bake a cake but just can't find time to make one from scratch, those in the Busy Baker section will help solve this problem. They are quick and easy yet capture the fabulous flavors of from-scratch cakes.

The versatile pound cake will always remain popular because it is so easy to accessorize. Although it is great served as is, if you want to fancy it up a bit, top it with strawberries and whipped cream or serve it with a rich dessert sauce. You can even make a dessert sandwich out of it by spreading a little of your favorite frosting between two thin slices. It can also be turned into a not-so-sweet treat by spreading a slice with cream cheese. I like to spread a slice with butter and pop it under the broiler for just a few seconds. The toasted pound cake slices can be served for breakfast or as a snack later in the day.

Southern Heritage Cakes

—◦◦◦◦◦◦◦◦◦◦▷◉◁◦◦◦◦◦◦◦◦◦◦—

Multilayer Cakes

OTHER CAKES

Multilayer Cakes

------◆◈◆------

FRESH COCONUT CAKE

Yield: 14 to 16 servings

*W*hen I was young, I enjoyed watching my mother as she cracked open a fresh coconut. After opening the "eyes" with a nail and hammer, she would drain the liquid into a glass. The coconut would then be placed into a 200- to 250-degree oven for about 20 minutes. This made it easier to get the edible part of the coconut out of the hard shell. A few knocks with the hammer and the shell would crack open. After peeling and grating the coconut, she would make one of the best coconut cakes I have ever tasted. Her original icing was made like divinity candy and the freshly grated coconut was sprinkled all over the cake. In later years, a simple 7-minute icing replaced the more difficult divinity type. I have been unable to find my mother's recipe, but have tried to duplicate it from my memory bank of flavor.

CAKE LAYERS

¼ pound (1 stick) butter or margarine
½ cup shortening
2 cups sugar
3 egg yolks
3 cups all-purpose flour
1 tablespoon baking powder
¼ teaspoon salt
1 cup milk
1½ teaspoons vanilla extract
5 egg whites

COCONUT FROSTING

2 egg whites
2 teaspoons light corn syrup
1½ cups sugar

⅓ cup of the liquid drained from fresh coconut
1 teaspoon vanilla extract
1 fresh coconut, peeled and grated (about 3½ cups)

Preheat the oven to 350 degrees F. Grease and flour three 9-inch cake pans.

In a large bowl, cream together the butter, shortening, and sugar. Add the egg yolks, one at a time, beating well after each addition.

In a medium bowl, combine the flour, baking powder, and salt. Stir to mix. Add the flour mixture to the creamed mixture alternately with the milk, starting and ending with the flour. Add the vanilla; mix well.

Beat the egg whites until stiff peaks form. Fold into the batter.

Divide the batter evenly among the prepared pans. Bake for 20 to 25 minutes, or until a wooden pick comes out clean when inserted into the center of the layers. Remove from pans immediately and cool completely on racks, before frosting.

To make the frosting, combine the egg whites, corn syrup, sugar, and coconut liquid in the top of a double boiler. Beat with an electric mixer for about 1 minute, until well mixed. Place over boiling water. Cook for 7 minutes, beating continuously with the electric mixer. The frosting should be thick and glossy. Remove from the heat and stir in the vanilla.

Spread the frosting on one cooled cake layer and sprinkle generously with grated coconut. Repeat with the second and third layers. Spread the frosting around the sides of the cake and cover with coconut.

NOTE: Leftover egg yolks can be used in baked custards or in cream pie fillings. Egg yolks can be frozen if stabilized with salt or sugar. If you plan to use them in savory dishes, add 1 teaspoon salt for each cup of yolks. If you plan to use them in sweet dishes, add 1 tablespoon sugar for each cup of yolks. Be sure to mark the container *sweet* or *savory*.

TOASTED COCONUT CAKE

Yield: 16 servings

Coconut is a flavor favorite with our family. Add coconut to a dessert and it immediately becomes a hit. Toasting the coconut adds a little crunch and also a unique flavor. This cake is meant to be made with the kind of coconut you can buy in bags or cans at the supermarket. Don't use fresh or frozen coconut because it is too moist.

CAKE LAYERS

2 cups coconut (canned or in plastic bags)
4 eggs, separated
½ pound (2 sticks) butter or margarine
2 cups sugar
1 teaspoon vanilla extract
½ teaspoon coconut-flavored extract
2 cups all-purpose flour
1 teaspoon baking soda
¼ teaspoon salt
1 cup buttermilk

TOASTED COCONUT FROSTING

8 ounces cream cheese, softened at room temperature
4 tablespoons butter or margarine
1 (16 oz.) box confectioners' sugar
Remaining 1 cup toasted coconut

Preheat the oven to 350 degrees F. Grease and lightly flour three 9-inch cake pans.

Spread the coconut in an ungreased jelly-roll pan (10x15x1 inch) or pan of approximate size. Toast in the oven for 3 to 4 minutes, until the coconut begins to brown slightly, stirring about every 30 seconds to prevent the coconut from getting too dark. When done, immediately remove the coconut from the pan to prevent further browning.

In a medium bowl, beat the egg whites until stiff but not dry. Set aside. In a large mixing bowl, beat together the butter, sugar, vanilla extract, and coconut flavoring. Add the egg yolks, one at a time, beating well after each addition.

In a small bowl, combine the flour, baking soda, and salt. Stir to mix. Add to the creamed mixture alternately with the buttermilk, starting and ending with the flour mixture. Fold in the beaten egg whites and 1 cup of the toasted coconut. Divide the batter evenly among the prepared pans. Bake for about 25 minutes, or until a wooden pick inserted in the center of the layers comes out clean. Remove from the pans and cool completely on a rack.

To make the frosting, combine the cream cheese, butter, and confectioners' sugar in a large mixing bowl. Beat until well mixed and smooth. Stir in the toasted coconut. Spread between the layers, on top of the cake, and around the sides of the cake.

NOTE: To make the cake even more beautiful, toast an extra cup of coconut and press it onto the sides of the frosted cake.

GRANNY'S SPECKLED
COCONUT CAKE

Yield: 14 to 16 servings

*A*s children, we referred to Granny's coconut cake as a "gray" cake because the icing was not as snow white as it is on the "traditional" coconut cake. After getting the coconut out of the hard shell, my grandmother would grind the unpeeled coconut. The brown part gave the coconut its speckled appearance. As much as I believe that the food processor is an indispensable appliance, it is not the tool of choice for this cake. An old-fashioned food grinder that you attach to the table with a clamp is best. The coconut seems moister when the food grinder is used. But if you don't have a grinder, use your food processor. The coconut must be chopped fine. If you can keep the cake around for a day or two, it will get better and better. Of course, it is so good that it might not last that long. When making this cake, remember to reserve the liquid that comes from the fresh coconut because it will be used in the frosting.

CAKE LAYERS

1 cup shortening
1¾ cups sugar
1 teaspoon vanilla extract
3 eggs
3 cups self-rising flour
1 cup milk

SPECKLED COCONUT FROSTING

1 cup sugar
3 tablespoons all-purpose flour
Coconut liquid plus enough milk to equal 1½ cups
4 tablespoons butter or margarine
3½ to 4 cups "speckled" coconut (see headnote)

Preheat the oven to 350 degrees F. Grease and flour three 9-inch cake pans.

Cream together the shortening and sugar. Add the vanilla. Mix well. Add the eggs, one at a time, beating well after each addition. Add the flour to the creamed mixture, alternately with the milk. Beat well. Divide evenly among the prepared pans. Bake for 20 to 25 minutes, or until a wooden pick comes out clean when inserted into the center of the layers. Cool completely on racks before frosting.

To make the frosting, combine all the frosting ingredients in a large heavy saucepan. Bring to a boil. Reduce heat to medium-high and cook for 5 to 7 minutes, stirring continuously, until thickened. Remove from heat and cool before frosting the layers. Spread the frosting between the layers and on top and sides of cake.

LADY BALTIMORE CAKE

Yield: 16 to 18 servings

*T*his elegant cake is only half of a royal pair. The other is the Lord Baltimore cake. At Christmastime, Mother always made a Lady Baltimore cake, which uses the whites of 8 eggs. She couldn't waste all those yolks so the perfect solution was to make the Lord Baltimore cake, which calls for 8 egg yolks. There are many variations for the Lady Baltimore icing. As I remember, Mother usually put some candied fruits and nuts in hers, but some earlier recipes call for fresh figs.

CAKE LAYERS

3 cups all-purpose flour
3 teaspoons baking powder
1/4 teaspoon salt
12 tablespoons (1½ sticks) butter or margarine, softened at
    room temperature
1¾ cups sugar
1 teaspoon vanilla extract
½ teaspoon almond extract
1 cup milk
5 egg whites

FROSTING

3 cups sugar
1 cup water
1 tablespoon light corn syrup
1/4 teaspoon cream of tartar
3 egg whites
3/4 cup raisins
½ cup chopped pecans
½ cup chopped almonds
1/3 cup chopped candied cherries
1/3 cup chopped fresh figs (optional)

Preheat the oven to 350 degrees F. Grease and lightly flour three 9-inch cake pans.

In a medium bowl, combine the flour, baking powder, and salt. Stir to mix. In a large mixing bowl, cream together the butter and sugar, beating well. Add the vanilla and almond extracts. Mix well. Add the flour mixture to the creamed mixture alternately with the milk, starting and ending with the flour.

In a medium bowl, beat the egg whites until stiff peaks form. Fold into the batter. Divide evenly among the prepared pans. Bake for about 25 minutes, or until a wooden pick inserted in the center of the layers comes out clean. Remove from pans immediately and cool on racks.

To make the frosting, combine the sugar, water, corn syrup, and cream of tartar in a medium saucepan. Cook over medium-high heat until mixture forms a thread when a small amount is dropped from a spoon, or to 248 degrees on a candy thermometer.

While syrup is cooking, beat the egg whites until stiff. When the syrup is ready, gradually add it to beaten egg whites, beating continuously on high speed until the mixture is thick enough to spread on cake. Stir in the raisins, pecans, almonds, candied cherries, and figs. Spread the frosting between the layers, on top, and around sides of cake.

LORD BALTIMORE CAKE

Yield: 16 to 18 servings

*T*his golden cake is highlighted with a fluffy white frosting filled with nuts, fruits, and macaroon crumbs.

CAKE LAYERS

3 cups all-purpose flour
4 teaspoons baking powder
¼ teaspoon salt
12 tablespoons (1½ sticks) butter or margarine, softened at
    room temperature
1½ cups sugar
8 egg yolks
⅔ cup milk
½ teaspoon pure lemon extract
1 teaspoon vanilla extract

FROSTING

3 cups sugar
1 cup water
¼ teaspoon cream of tartar
1 teaspoon light corn syrup
3 egg whites
1 cup chopped pecans
1 cup raisins
½ cup coconut macaroon crumbs

Preheat the oven to 350 degrees F. Grease and lightly flour three 9-inch cake pans.

Combine the flour, baking powder, and salt in a medium bowl. Stir to mix. In a large bowl, cream together the butter and sugar. Add the egg yolks, one at a time, beating well after each addition. Add the flour mixture to the creamed mixture alternately with the milk, starting and ending with the flour. Add the lemon and vanilla extracts and mix well. Divide the batter evenly among the prepared pans. Bake for 25 to 30 minutes, or until a wooden pick inserted in the center of the layers comes out clean. Remove from pans immediately and cool on racks.

To prepare the frosting, combine the sugar, water, cream of tartar, and corn syrup. Cook over medium-high heat until a small amount dropped from a spoon forms a thread, or to 248 degrees on a candy thermometer.

While the syrup is cooking, beat the egg whites until stiff. When the syrup has reached the thread stage, gradually add it to the egg whites, beating continuously until the mixture is thick enough to spread on cake. Stir in pecans, raisins, and macaroon crumbs. Spread between layers, on top, and around sides of cake.

STRAWBERRY SHORTCAKE

Yield: 16 servings

*W*hen I was growing up, strawberry shortcake meant two of Mother's homemade cake layers, with strawberries and sugar between the layers and on top. The strawberry juice would seep into the layers and drizzle down the sides of the cake. Simple but oh so good! At our house, we consider a slice of pound cake topped with sweetened strawberries and whipped cream as strawberry shortcake. I know that this is not what many people think of when shortcake is mentioned, so the following recipe features the biscuit-type shortcake, if you prefer.

1 quart strawberries, cleaned and sliced
1⅓ cups plus 1 tablespoon sugar
2 cups all-purpose flour
3 teaspoons baking powder
¼ teaspoon salt
⅓ cup shortening
⅔ cup milk
1 tablespoon butter or margarine, melted
1 cup heavy cream, sweetened and whipped (optional)

Combine the strawberries with 1⅓ cups of the sugar. Stir and let sit until sugar dissolves and forms a light syrup.   *(continued)*

Preheat the oven to 400 degrees F. Grease two 8- or 9-inch cake pans.

In a large bowl, combine the flour, baking powder, salt, and remaining 1 tablespoon sugar. Stir to mix. Cut the shortening into the flour mixture until it is the consistency of coarse cornmeal. Add the milk and mix well. Divide the dough into two equal portions and pat each into one of the prepared pans. Brush each shortcake with melted butter. Bake for 18 to 20 minutes, until lightly browned. Remove from pans and cool completely on racks before adding the strawberries.

When shortcakes are cool, spoon sweetened strawberries between the layers and on top of the shortcake. Serve with sweetened whipped cream, if desired.

PLANTATION FUDGE CAKE

Yield: 14 to 16 servings

Nothing soothes the Southern palate quite like a big slice of chocolate cake. The combination of melted chocolate, butter, and confectioners' sugar gives the frosting a "cooked" appearance and texture. The frosting tastes like walnut fudge.

CAKE LAYERS

¼ pound (1 stick) butter or margarine, softened at room temperature
2 cups sugar
3 squares semisweet chocolate, melted
3 eggs
1 teaspoon vanilla extract
2¼ cups all-purpose flour
½ teaspoon salt
1½ teaspoons baking soda
1¼ cups buttermilk

CHOCOLATE NUT FROSTING

2 squares semisweet chocolate
¼ pound (1 stick) butter or margarine
1 (16 oz.) box confectioners' sugar
1 teaspoon vanilla extract
¼ cup milk
½ cup chopped walnuts

Preheat the oven to 350 degrees F. Grease and lightly flour two 9-inch cake pans.

Combine the butter, sugar, and melted chocolate in a large mixing bowl. Beat until well mixed. Add the eggs one at a time, beating well after each addition. Add vanilla. Mix well.

In a medium bowl, combine the flour, salt, and baking soda. Stir to mix. Add to the creamed mixture alternately with the buttermilk, starting and ending with the flour mixture. Divide the batter evenly between the prepared pans.

Bake for 30 to 35 minutes, or until a wooden pick inserted in the center of the layers comes out clean. Remove from the pans immediately and cool on a rack.

To make the frosting, melt the chocolate and butter together in a saucepan over medium-low heat or in the microwave. Pour into a large mixing bowl. Add confectioners' sugar, vanilla extract, and milk. Beat until smooth. Stir in walnuts.

When cake layers are completely cool, spread frosting between layers, on top, and around sides of cake.

NOTE: If the frosting becomes too thick, add a small amount of milk and stir until mixed.

VELVET FUDGE CAKE

Yield: 14 to 16 servings

"Velvet" is the perfect description for the texture of these light chocolate layers sandwiched together with vanilla cream and covered with a light and creamy fudge frosting. Sure to be a favorite with young and old alike.

CAKE LAYERS

2¼ cups all-purpose flour
¼ cup cocoa
1 teaspoon baking soda
½ teaspoon salt
1½ cups sugar
1 cup sour cream
1 teaspoon white vinegar
¾ cup vegetable oil
1 teaspoon vanilla extract
2 eggs

VANILLA CREAM FILLING

4 tablespoons butter, softened at room temperature
1 cup confectioners' sugar
½ teaspoon vanilla extract

FUDGE FROSTING

¼ pound (1 stick) butter, softened at room temperature
5 tablespoons milk
1 teaspoon vanilla extract
3 to 3½ cups confectioners' sugar
⅓ cup cocoa

Preheat the oven to 350 degrees F. Grease and lightly flour two 9-inch cake pans.

Combine all the ingredients for the layers in a large mixing bowl. Beat for 2 to 3 minutes. Batter should be thick but smooth. Divide the batter evenly between the prepared pans. Bake for about 20 minutes, or until a wooden pick inserted in the center of the layers comes out clean. Cool completely on racks.

Combine the filling ingredients in a medium mixing bowl. Beat until light and creamy. Spread between the cooled layers.

Combine the frosting ingredients in a large mixing bowl. Beat until light and creamy. Spread over top and around sides of cake. If the frosting seems too thin, simply add additional confectioners' sugar. If it should get too thick, add a little milk.

LEMON CHEESE CAKE

Yield: about 16 servings

This lemony delight has been on the Southern dessert menu for many years. The name is confusing because there is actually no cheese in it. It was only after spending some time in New York City that I realized what Southerners have been referring to as lemon cheese is almost identical to lemon curd.

CAKE LAYERS

4 egg whites
⅔ cup shortening
1½ cups sugar
1 teaspoon vanilla extract
2½ cups all-purpose flour
3 teaspoons baking powder
¼ teaspoon salt
1 cup ice water

LEMON CHEESE ICING

3 egg yolks
1 cup sugar
¼ pound (1 stick) butter or margarine, softened at room temperature
⅓ cup freshly squeezed lemon juice
1½ to 2 cups coconut (canned or in plastic bags)

Preheat the oven to 350 degrees F. Grease and lightly flour the bottoms of two 9-inch cake pans.

(continued)

Beat the egg whites until stiff but not dry. In a large bowl, combine the shortening, sugar, and vanilla extract. Beat until well mixed.

In a medium bowl, combine the flour, baking powder, and salt. Stir to mix. Add to the creamed mixture alternately with the ice water. Fold in the beaten egg whites. Divide the batter evenly between the prepared pans and bake for 18 to 20 minutes, or until a wooden pick inserted in the center of the layers comes out clean. Cool completely on a rack.

For the icing, combine the egg yolks, sugar, softened butter, and lemon juice in the top of a double boiler. Mix well. Place over boiling water. Cook, stirring continuously, for about 10 minutes, until the lemon cheese is smooth and will coat the back of a spoon. It will thicken more as it cools. Place the pan in a larger pan or bowl of cold water to speed up thickening.

Spread the icing between the cake layers and on top of the cake. To keep the outer edges of the cake layers soft, you might also want to spread a little of the icing around the sides of the cake. Sprinkle the top (and sides, if desired) with coconut.

Carrot Date Cake

Yield: about 16 servings

Carrot cake has become a classic in our country. There are many different versions from simple ones using baby food carrots to unusual ones like chocolate carrot cake. My newest carrot cake recipe has the added flavor of dates, pineapple, and ground ginger.

CAKE LAYERS
2½ cups all-purpose flour
2 teaspoons baking soda
1 teaspoon ground cinnamon
¼ teaspoon ground ginger
½ teaspoon salt
1 cup dates (do not use the sugared ones)
1½ cups finely grated carrots (about 3 medium carrots)

1 cup chopped pecans
¾ cup vegetable oil
2 cups firmly packed light brown sugar
4 eggs, separated
1 teaspoon vanilla extract
1 cup buttermilk
1 (8 oz.) can crushed pineapple, well drained

PINEAPPLE–CREAM CHEESE FROSTING

1 (8 oz.) container pineapple-flavored cream cheese
¼ pound (1 stick) butter or margarine, softened at room temperature
1 (16 oz.) box confectioners' sugar
1 cup chopped pecans

Preheat the oven to 350 degrees F. Grease and lightly flour three 9-inch cake pans. In a medium bowl, combine 2 cups of the flour with the baking soda, cinnamon, ginger, and salt. Stir to mix. Put the remaining ½ cup flour and the dates in the bowl of a food processor fitted with the steel blade. Process until the dates are about the size of raisins. Remove the floured dates to a medium bowl. Add the carrots and pecans. Toss lightly to mix.

In a large mixing bowl, combine the oil and brown sugar. Beat until well mixed. Add the egg yolks one at a time, beating well after each addition. Add the vanilla. Mix well. Add the flour mixture alternately with the buttermilk, starting and ending with the flour. Stir in the carrot mixture and the drained pineapple.

Beat the egg whites until stiff but not dry. Fold into the batter. Divide the batter evenly among the prepared pans. Bake for 25 to 30 minutes, or until a wooden pick comes out clean when inserted in the center of the cake. Remove from the pans and cool completely on a rack.

To make the frosting, beat together the cream cheese and butter in a large bowl. Add the confectioners' sugar. Beat until smooth. Stir in the pecans. Spread between cake layers and on the top and sides of cake.

Sweet Caroline Cake

Yield: 14 servings

This cake is a slight variation of a recipe that I developed for a special little girl named Caroline. I learned of her allergy to milk and eggs when her grandmother called to see if I had a recipe for a cake without these two ingredients. She explained that her granddaughter would not be able to enjoy her first birthday cake unless she could find a recipe without eggs or milk. I couldn't find one in my files so I decided to develop one. This cake is so flavorful that even those without an allergy to these products will want to add it to their list of favorite desserts. The grandmother made the cake using my recipe and sent some photos showing Caroline enjoying her cake. Now I know the true meaning of the old saying, "a picture is worth a thousand words."

¼ pound (1 stick) margarine
¾ cup sugar
¼ cup firmly packed light brown sugar
2 cups self-rising flour
½ teaspoon ground cinnamon
1 cup cold, unsweetened apple juice
1 teaspoon vanilla extract
Nondairy topping or sweetened whipped cream (optional)

Preheat the oven to 350 degrees F. Grease and flour two 8-inch cake pans. Cut a circle of parchment or wax paper to fit the bottoms. Grease the paper.

In a large bowl, cream together the margarine and both sugars. Beat until very smooth. Combine the flour and cinnamon in a small bowl. Stir to mix. Add the flour to the creamed mixture alternately with the apple juice, starting and ending with the flour. Add the vanilla. Mix well. Divide the batter evenly between the prepared pans. Bake for 18 to 20 minutes, or until the cake pulls away from the sides of the pans.

This is a very delicate cake so be careful when removing from the pans. Turn out onto a rack. Remove the paper. When the cake is completely cooled, carefully remove the rack. Frost with nondairy whipped topping or sweetened whipped cream.

PINEAPPLE CAKE

Yield: about 16 servings

$\mathcal{M}$y mother-in-law makes a wonderful pineapple cake and this is a Hilburn family favorite. It was a hit with me after the first bite.

CAKE LAYERS

5 egg whites
¼ pound (1 stick) unsalted butter, softened at room temperature
1 cup sugar
1 teaspoon vanilla extract
2 cups all-purpose flour
2 teaspoons baking powder
¼ teaspoon salt
1 cup ice water

PINEAPPLE TOPPING

1 (20 oz.) can crushed pineapple, well drained
1½ cups sugar
4 tablespoons butter
1 cup heavy cream, sweetened and whipped (optional)

Preheat the oven to 350 degrees F. Grease and lightly flour two 9-inch cake pans.

Beat the egg whites until stiff. Set aside. In a large bowl, cream together the butter, sugar, and vanilla extract. Combine flour, baking powder, and salt. Add to creamed mixture alternately with the ice water, starting and ending with flour mixture. Fold in the egg whites.

Divide evenly between the prepared pans and bake for 20 to 25 minutes, or until a wooden pick comes out clean when inserted into the center of the layers. Remove from pans and cool on racks.

To make the topping, combine the drained pineapple and sugar in a medium saucepan. Cook over medium-high heat until the mixture begins to thicken slightly. Don't overcook or it will become syrupy. Stir in the butter. Cool before spreading between layers and on top of cake. If desired, spread whipped cream around the sides of the cake just before serving.

BLACK WALNUT CAKE

Yield: about 16 servings

*W*hen I was a youngster, Mother baked a black walnut or a hickory nut (called "hicker nut" by many Southerners) cake at Christmastime. Hickory nuts are not as plentiful as they were back then and even if they were, I think I would use black walnuts. Both are extremely hard to get out of their shells, but black walnuts can be purchased already shelled and chopped.

CAKE LAYERS

5 eggs, separated
½ pound (2 sticks) butter or margarine, softened at room temperature
2 cups sugar
1 teaspoon vanilla extract
2¼ cups all-purpose flour
1 teaspoon baking soda
¼ teaspoon salt
1 cup buttermilk
1 cup chopped black walnuts

BLACK WALNUT FROSTING

¼ pound (1 stick) butter or margarine, softened at room temperature
1 teaspoon vanilla extract
2 tablespoons milk
3 to 3½ cups confectioners' sugar
1 cup chopped black walnuts

Preheat the oven to 350 degrees F. Grease and lightly flour three 9-inch cake pans.

In a large mixing bowl, beat the egg whites until stiff. Set aside. In another bowl, cream the butter and sugar. Add the egg yolks, one at a time, beating well after each addition. Add the vanilla. Mix well.

Combine the flour, baking soda, and salt in a medium bowl. Stir to mix. Add to the creamed mixture alternately with the buttermilk. Mix well. Stir in the black walnuts. Fold in the egg whites.

Divide the batter evenly among the prepared pans. Bake for 20 to 25 minutes, or until a wooden pick comes out clean when inserted into the center of the layers. Remove from the pans immediately. Cool completely on racks.

To make the frosting, combine the butter, vanilla, milk, and 2 cups of the sugar in a large bowl. Beat until creamy. Gradually add remaining sugar until mixture is thick enough to spread smoothly. Stir in the black walnuts. Spread frosting between layers, on top and sides of cake.

DRIED APPLE STACK CAKE

Yield: 14 to 16 servings

The dried apple stack cake recipe has been passed down from generation to generation in the South. Although commercially prepared dried apples can be used in this recipe, the cake will not taste the same as the original cake my grandmother made. I remember Mother drying her apples on a screen my daddy had made for her. She spread the sliced apples on the screen and covered them with a snow-white cloth. The screen was placed in the sun until the apples were dried. These apples, when cooked, would be much darker than those available at the supermarket, which are usually treated with chemicals to preserve their light color. The thin layers for this cake are made with sorghum syrup, but unsulfured molasses can be substituted. It is not unusual for this cake to have as many as six layers, but the following recipe has only three.

¼ pound (1 stick) butter or margarine, softened at room temperature
¾ cup firmly packed light brown sugar
¾ cup sorghum syrup or unsulfured molasses
2 eggs
½ cup buttermilk
½ teaspoon baking soda
2½ cups all-purpose flour
½ teaspoon ground cinnamon
4½ cups cooked dried apples (see note)
½ cup sugar

Preheat the oven to 350 degrees F. Grease and lightly flour three 9-inch cake pans.

(continued)

In a large mixing bowl, cream together the butter, brown sugar, and sorghum syrup. Add the eggs. Beat until well mixed. Combine the buttermilk and baking soda in a small bowl. Combine the flour and cinnamon in a medium bowl. Stir to mix.

Add the flour mixture to the creamed mixture alternately with the buttermilk mixture, starting and ending with the flour. Divide the batter evenly among the prepared cake pans, using about 1⅛ cups per pan. Bake for about 15 minutes, or until a wooden pick comes out clean when inserted into the center of the layers. Remove from the pans and cool on a rack.

Combine the cooked apples with the sugar. Stir to mix. Spoon about 1½ cups of the apples between each layer and on top of the cake.

NOTE: To yield 4½ cups cooked dried apples, combine 12 ounces dried apples with 4½ cups water in a medium saucepan. Bring to a boil, reduce heat to medium, and cook for 5 to 7 minutes, until apples have absorbed the water.

BLACKBERRY JAM CAKE

Yield: about 16 servings

*T*his old Southern favorite is best if wrapped in foil and stored for at least two days before slicing.

CAKE LAYERS
½ pound (2 sticks) butter or margarine, softened at room temperature
2 cups sugar
5 eggs
3 cups all-purpose flour
1 teaspoon baking soda
1 teaspoon ground cloves
¼ teaspoon grated nutmeg
½ teaspoon ground cinnamon
1 cup buttermilk
1 cup seedless blackberry jam
1 cup chopped pecans
1 cup raisins

CARAMEL ICING

1 cup sugar
1 cup firmly packed light brown sugar
¼ pound (1 stick) butter or margarine, softened at room temperature
2 tablespoons light corn syrup
1 cup buttermilk
½ teaspoon baking soda

Preheat the oven to 350 degrees F. Grease three 9-inch cake pans. Line the bottoms of the pans with wax paper cut to fit and then grease and lightly flour the paper.

In a large bowl, cream together the butter and sugar. Add the eggs one at a time, beating well with each addition.

Combine the flour, baking soda, cloves, nutmeg, and cinnamon in a medium bowl. Stir to mix. Add to the creamed mixture alternately with the buttermilk. Mix well. Add the jam. Mix until blended. Stir in the pecans and raisins. Divide evenly among the prepared pans. Bake for 30 to 35 minutes, or until a wooden pick inserted into the center of the layers comes out clean. Remove from the pans immediately. Remove the wax paper. Cool completely on a rack.

For the icing, combine the sugar, brown sugar, butter, and corn syrup in a heavy saucepan. Place the buttermilk in a 2-cup container and add the baking soda, which will foam up. Add the buttermilk mixture to the saucepan. Mix well. Cook over medium-low heat until the mixture reaches the "soft ball" stage —drop a little of the icing in a cup of cold water; if you can form it into a soft ball, remove from heat. Beat to spreading consistency. Spread between layers and on top and sides of cake.

MAMA'S LANE CAKE

Yield: about 16 servings

*T*he original version of this classic Southern cake has been credited to another Alabamian by the name of Emma Rylander Lane. Over the years, this wonderful cake has weathered numerous makeovers and has always come out rich and beautiful. Many versions of the fruit- and nut-filled icing call for bourbon, brandy, or rum, but being from the Bible Belt, my mother never used liquor in her Lane cake. At Christmastime Mama always made about a dozen cakes and the Lane cake was one of the family favorites. She seldom used recipes for her cakes, so I have tried to duplicate the Lane Cake as I remember hers.

CAKE LAYERS

8 egg whites
½ pound (2 sticks) butter or margarine, softened at room temperature
1¾ cups sugar
1½ teaspoons vanilla extract
3¼ cups all-purpose flour
1 tablespoon baking powder
¼ teaspoon salt
1 cup milk

ICING

12 tablespoons (1½ sticks) butter or margarine, melted
1 cup sugar
8 egg yolks
¼ cup milk
1 teaspoon vanilla extract
½ cup chopped raisins
1 cup chopped pecans
1 cup coconut (canned or in plastic bags)
¾ cup chopped candied cherries

Preheat the oven to 350 degrees F. Grease three 9-inch cake pans on the bottom only. Line the bottoms with wax paper cut to fit and grease the paper and lightly dust with flour.

In a large mixing bowl, beat the egg whites until stiff. Set aside. In another mixing bowl, cream together the butter and sugar. Add the vanilla. Mix well.

Combine the flour, baking powder, and salt in a third bowl. Stir to mix. Add the flour mixture to the creamed mixture alternately with the milk. Mix well. Fold in the beaten egg whites. Pour about 2½ cups of the batter into each pan. Smooth the tops. Bake for 20 minutes, or until a wooden pick comes out clean when inserted into the center of each cake. Remove from pans immediately. Remove paper. Cool completely on rack before frosting.

To make the icing, combine the melted butter, sugar, and egg yolks in a heavy saucepan. Mix well. Stir in the milk. Place over medium-high heat and cook until mixture begins to thicken. This should take 3 to 4 minutes. Remove from the heat. Stir in the vanilla extract. Add the fruits and nuts. Mix well. Spread between layers, on top, and around sides.

PEANUT BUTTER CAKE

Yield: 16 servings

*T*he first time I tasted peanut butter cake was at a dinner at my in-laws' home. I like just about anything that has peanut butter in it so this cake was a hit with the first bite. The creamy, simple-to-make peanut butter frosting is spread on yellow cake layers. That's all there is to it!

CAKE LAYERS

¼ pound (1 stick) butter or margarine, softened at room temperature
½ cup shortening
2 cups sugar
4 eggs
3 cups all-purpose flour
¼ teaspoon salt
1½ teaspoons baking soda
1 cup buttermilk
1 teaspoon vanilla extract

PEANUT BUTTER ICING

2 cups sugar
1 cup milk
2 tablespoons light corn syrup
1 tablespoon butter or margarine
1¼ cups peanut butter
1 teaspoon vanilla extract

Preheat the oven to 350 degrees F. Grease and lightly flour three 9-inch cake pans.

In a large mixing bowl, cream together the butter, shortening, and sugar. Add the eggs one at a time, beating well after each addition. Combine the flour, salt, and baking soda in a medium bowl. Stir to mix. Add to the creamed mixture alternately with the buttermilk. Beat well. Add the vanilla. Mix well. Divide the batter evenly among the prepared pans. Bake for about 25 minutes, or until a wooden pick comes out clean when inserted into the center of the layers. Cool completely on a rack.

To make the icing, combine the sugar, milk, and corn syrup in a heavy saucepan. Bring to a boil and cook for 3 minutes. Remove from the heat and place the pan in a larger pan of cold water. Add the butter, peanut butter, and vanilla. Beat until the mixture thickens to a spreading consistency. Spread the icing between the layers and on the top and sides of the cake.

NOTE: If the icing thickens too much, add a little milk. If it fails to thicken, add a little confectioners' sugar.

Single-Layer Cakes

••••••••••••◦)) ✹ ((◦••••••••••••

DEVIL'S FOOD CAKE

....

Yield: about 15 servings

*T*o most Southerners, devil's food cake means dark chocolate layers with white icing. This cake layer is moist with a tender crumb. One icing is a home-style buttercream. The old traditional Southern devil's food cake had a divinity icing, which is a little more trouble to make, but either one makes a great-tasting cake.

CAKE

½ pound (2 sticks) butter or margarine, softened at room temperature
1⅔ cups sugar
2 eggs
1 teaspoon vanilla extract
2½ cups all-purpose flour
¼ cup cocoa
1½ teaspoons baking soda
¼ teaspoon salt
1½ cups ice water

HOMESTYLE BUTTERCREAM ICING

¼ pound (1 stick) butter or margarine
½ teaspoon vanilla extract
1 (16 oz.) box confectioners' sugar
3 to 4 tablespoons water

DIVINITY ICING

2 cups sugar
¼ cup light corn syrup
⅓ cup water
⅛ teaspoon salt
2 egg whites
1 teaspoon vanilla extract

Preheat the oven to 350 degrees F. Grease and lightly flour a 9x13x2-inch baking pan.

In a large bowl, combine the butter and sugar. Beat well. Add the eggs and vanilla. Beat well.

In a medium bowl, combine the flour, cocoa, baking soda, and salt. Stir to mix. Add the flour mixture to the creamed mixture alternately with the ice water. Pour the batter into the prepared pan. Bake for 30 to 35 minutes, or until a wooden pick inserted into the center of the cake comes out clean. Cool completely on a rack before icing.

To make the butter cream icing, combine the butter, vanilla, and sugar. Beat until mixture starts to come together. Add the water, a tablespoon at a time, until the mixture becomes light and creamy. Spread over the top of the devil's food cake and around the sides.

To make the divinity icing, if desired, combine the sugar, corn syrup, water, and salt in a medium saucepan. Bring to a boil. Do not stir. Wash down the sides of the pan with a brush dipped in water, which prevents crystals from forming. Reduce heat to medium-high and cook until the mixture forms a thread when a small amount is dropped from a spoon, or until it reaches about 248 degrees F. on a candy thermometer.

While syrup is cooking, beat egg whites until stiff. When the syrup has reached the proper temperature, add it in a slow stream to the egg whites, beating constantly at high speed until the mixture is thick enough to spread on cake. Stir in vanilla extract.

JAPANESE FRUITCAKE SQUARES

Yield: 12 to 16 servings

Japanese fruitcake is a popular item on our holiday dessert menu, especially with my husband and our son-in-law, Freddy. The name has always intrigued me because there are no Japanese ingredients in the cake and it certainly doesn't look Japanese. A combination of fruit juices, spices, coconut, nuts, and raisins gives this cake its unique flavor. These cookielike cake squares are an updated version of this old cake. The taste is definitely the same, but the texture of the filling is similar to that of a pecan pie with a semicrisp topping of nuts and coconut.

CAKE

1 (18.25 ounce) box milk chocolate cake mix
1 teaspoon ground cinnamon
½ teaspoon ground cloves
1 egg
¼ pound (1 stick) butter or margarine, softened at room temperature
½ cup chopped pecans

FILLING

1 cup sugar
¼ pound (1 stick) butter or margarine, softened at room temperature
2 eggs
1 teaspoon finely grated orange peel
1 teaspoon finely grated lemon peel
2 tablespoons freshly squeezed orange juice
1 cup chopped pecans
1 cup coconut (canned or in plastic bags)
½ cup raisins

Preheat the oven to 350 degrees F. Grease a 9x13x2-inch baking pan.

In a large bowl, combine the cake mix, cinnamon, cloves, egg, butter, and pecans. Mix well. Press into the prepared pan. Bake for 15 minutes. Allow to cool slightly.

Mix the filling in a large bowl. Combine the sugar, butter, eggs, orange peel, lemon peel, and orange juice. Mix well. Stir in the pecans, coconut, and raisins. Carefully spoon this mixture over the cake. It is best to spoon small amounts and then lightly spread the mixture. Bake for 30 minutes. Place on a rack to cool. Cut into squares when completely cool.

PEAR-ADISE RAISIN NUT CAKE

Yield: 18 servings

*P*ears add a special moistness to this delicate cake. Ground pecans and raisins give the cake its unusual texture.

1 cup pecans
1 cup raisins
1 cup peeled chopped pears
3 eggs
1¼ cups vegetable oil
¾ cup sugar
1¼ cups firmly packed light brown sugar
2½ cups self-rising flour

CARAMEL GLAZE

4 tablespoons butter or margarine
½ cup firmly packed light brown sugar
⅓ cup sour cream

Preheat the oven to 350 degrees F. Grease and lightly flour a 9x13x2-inch baking pan.

Combine the pecans and raisins in the bowl of a food processor fitted with the steel blade. Process until very fine. Pour into a bowl and add the pears.

Combine the eggs, oil, sugar, and brown sugar in a large bowl. Beat until well blended. Gradually add the flour, beating well. Stir in the pear mixture. Pour into the prepared pan. Bake for 45 to 50 minutes, or until a wooden pick inserted in the center of the cake comes out clean. *(continued)*

While the cake bakes, make the glaze by combining the butter and brown sugar in a small saucepan. Bring to a boil. Cook, stirring constantly, for about 3 minutes. Remove from heat and stir in sour cream. Spoon over the warm cake.

STRAWBERRY RIBBON CAKE

Yield: about 20 servings

I had my grandson, Jesse, on my mind when I was developing this recipe. Strawberry cake is his favorite dessert. When his birthday rolls around, he always expects a strawberry cake to be on the table. Of course, I let him be one of my taste testers for this cake, and when I heard the yummy sounds he was making when he took that first bite, I knew the cake was a success.

CREAM CHEESE RIBBON

8 ounces cream cheese, softened at room temperature
1 tablespoon all-purpose flour
⅓ cup confectioners' sugar
1 egg
1 tablespoon milk
½ teaspoon vanilla extract

CAKE

3 eggs, separated
12 tablespoons (1½ sticks) butter or margarine, softened at room temperature
⅔ cup sugar
1 cup strawberry preserves
1 teaspoon vanilla extract
2 cups all-purpose flour
2 teaspoons baking soda
¼ teaspoon salt
½ cup buttermilk

STRAWBERRY FROSTING

3 ounces cream cheese, softened at room temperature
4 tablespoons butter or margarine
¼ cup strawberry preserves
1 (16 oz.) box confectioners' sugar
½ cup chopped walnuts

Combine all the cheese ribbon ingredients in a medium bowl. Beat until smooth.

Preheat the oven to 350 degrees F. Grease and flour a 9x13x2-inch baking pan.

Beat the egg whites until stiff but not dry. Set aside. In a large mixing bowl, cream together the butter, sugar, and strawberry preserves. Add the egg yolks and vanilla. Beat well.

In a medium bowl, combine the flour, baking soda, and salt. Add to the creamed mixture alternately with the buttermilk, starting and ending with the flour mixture. Fold in the beaten egg whites. Pour about half the batter into the pan. Spoon cream cheese mixture over the batter and carefully spread with the back of the spoon. The cream cheese mixture does not have to cover the batter completely. Pour the remaining batter over the cream cheese ribbon. Spread to cover. Bake for 30 to 40 minutes, until the cake springs back when lightly touched in the center. Cool completely in the pan before frosting.

While the cake bakes, make the frosting. Combine the cream cheese, butter, and strawberry preserves in a large mixing bowl. Beat until well mixed. Add the confectioners' sugar. Beat until smooth. Stir in the walnuts. Spread on top of cooled cake.

UPSIDE-DOWN
PINEAPPLE GINGERBREAD

Yield: about 8 servings

*T*his simple cake combines two old Southern favorites—gingerbread and pineapple upside-down cake. No sauce is needed for the gingerbread because the pineapple topping bakes along with the cake.

TOPPING

2 tablespoons butter or margarine
¼ cup firmly packed light brown sugar
1 cup well-drained crushed pineapple (reserve the juice)

CAKE

1¾ cups all-purpose flour
¾ cup unsulfured molasses
¼ cup sugar
3 tablespoons reserved pineapple juice
⅓ cup hot water
5½ tablespoons butter or margarine, softened at room temperature
1 egg
¾ teaspoon baking soda
¾ teaspoon ground ginger
½ teaspoon ground cinnamon
¼ teaspoon salt
1 cup heavy cream, sweetened and whipped (optional)

Preheat the oven to 350 degrees F.

Melt the 2 tablespoons butter in a 7x11-inch baking pan. Sprinkle the brown sugar over the butter. Spoon the pineapple over the brown sugar mixture.

In a large bowl, combine all the cake ingredients except the heavy cream. Mix until well blended. Pour over pineapple mixture. Bake for about 25 minutes, or until a wooden pick inserted in the center of the cake comes out clean. Invert immediately onto a serving plate. Serve with a dollop of whipped cream, if desired.

TOPSY-TURVY PINEAPPLE CAKE

Yield: about 8 servings

This is just a cute name for an old favorite, pineapple upside-down cake. It is so simple to make that it could easily be a Busy Baker cake. The pineapple flavor is enhanced by the addition of pineapple juice in the cake layers.

7 tablespoons butter or margarine, at room temperature
2/3 cup firmly packed light brown sugar
1 (8 oz.) can sliced pineapple, drained, juice reserved
1¼ cups all-purpose flour
¾ cup sugar
1½ teaspoons baking powder
¼ teaspoon salt
1/3 cup reserved pineapple juice
2 tablespoons milk
2 egg whites
½ teaspoon vanilla extract

Preheat the oven to 350 degrees F.

Melt 3 tablespoons of the butter in an 8-inch, 2-inch deep iron skillet or cake pan. Sprinkle the brown sugar over the melted butter. Place the 4 pineapple slices in the pan, pushing them gently into the brown sugar mixture.

In a large mixing bowl, combine the flour, sugar, baking powder, salt, remaining 4 tablespoons butter, pineapple juice, and milk. Beat until well mixed. Add the egg whites and vanilla. Beat until smooth. Pour into the prepared pan and bake for 30 to 35 minutes, or until a wooden pick inserted in the center of the cake comes out clean. Invert immediately onto a cake plate. If any of the pineapple slices stick to the bottom of the pan, gently remove them and place them on top of the cake.

CHOCOLATE-COVERED CHERRY CAKE

Yield: 15 to 18 servings

This light cherry-speckled cake will quickly become a favorite with anyone who likes chocolate-covered cherries. One taste tester remarked that the cake "tastes elegant."

¼ *pound (1 stick) butter or margarine, softened at room temperature*
2 *cups sugar*
4 *eggs, separated*
2 *cups all-purpose flour*
2 *teaspoons baking powder*
1 *cup milk*
1 *cup chopped walnuts*
1 *cup chopped maraschino cherries (reserve juice for frosting)*

CHOCOLATE CHERRY FROSTING
¼ *pound (1 stick) butter or margarine*
3 *tablespoons cocoa*
6 *tablespoons maraschino cherry juice*
1 *teaspoon vanilla extract*
1 *(16 oz.) box confectioners' sugar*

Preheat the oven to 350 degrees F. Grease and lightly flour a 9x13x2-inch baking pan.

In a large mixing bowl, cream together the butter and sugar. Add the egg yolks one at a time, beating well after each addition. Combine the flour and baking powder in a small bowl. Stir to mix. Add to the creamed mixture alternately with the milk, starting and ending with the flour mixture. Stir in the walnuts and cherries.

Beat the egg whites until stiff but not dry. Fold into the batter. Pour into prepared pan. Bake for 40 to 45 minutes, or until a wooden pick comes out clean when inserted into the center of the cake.

While the cake bakes, make the frosting. Combine the butter, cocoa, and cherry juice in a medium saucepan. Cook over medium heat until the butter melts and the mixture is smooth. Remove from heat. Stir in vanilla. Add confectioners' sugar. Beat until smooth. Pour immediately over the warm cake and smooth with a spatula. Cool completely before slicing.

SELF-FROSTED HOLIDAY CAKE

Yield: 15 to 18 servings

*T*his is a version of an upside-down cake. The rich frosting that cooks right along with the cake is made with sweetened condensed milk, candied fruits, and nuts. It is colorful as well as tasty.

1 cup chopped candied cherries
¾ cup chopped candied pineapple
½ cup chopped pecans
¾ cup coconut (canned or in plastic bags)
1 (14 oz.) can sweetened condensed milk
¼ pound (1 stick) butter or margarine, softened at room temperature
1 cup sugar
3 eggs
1 teaspoon vanilla extract
¼ teaspoon rum extract
2 cups all-purpose flour
2 teaspoons baking powder
¼ teaspoon salt
1 cup milk
1 cup heavy cream, whipped (optional)

Preheat the oven to 350 degrees F. Line a 9x13x2-inch baking pan with aluminum foil. Butter the foil.

Combine the cherries, pineapple, pecans, and coconut in a medium bowl. Toss to mix. Sprinkle the fruit mixture in the bottom of the pan. Drizzle the condensed milk evenly over the fruit mixture.

(continued)

In a large mixing bowl, cream together the butter and sugar. Add the eggs one at a time, beating well with each addition. Add the vanilla and rum extracts. Mix just to blend.

In a medium bowl, combine the flour, baking powder, and salt. Stir to mix. Add to the creamed mixture alternately with the milk. Pour into the prepared pan. Bake for 20 to 25 minutes, or until the cake springs back when lightly touched in the center.

Remove from the oven and, if necessary, run a thin knife blade around the edge to loosen the cake. Carefully invert the cake onto the cake plate. Remove the foil. When the cake is completely cooled, frost the sides with whipped cream, if desired.

RUSSIAN TEA CAKE

Yield: about 15 servings

*U*nderneath the easy-to-make caramel icing is a light and tender spice cake flavored with instant tea mix and orange juice. Russian tea is a favorite beverage in the South and this cake is similar in flavor to the popular spiced tea.

CAKE

12 tablespoons (1½ sticks) butter or margarine, softened at room temperature
1¼ cups sugar
1 teaspoon vanilla extract
3 eggs
2 cups all-purpose flour
1 tablespoon baking powder
½ teaspoon salt
⅓ cup instant tea mix with sugar and lemon
1 teaspoon ground cinnamon
¼ teaspoon grated nutmeg
¼ teaspoon ground cloves
1 cup orange juice

EASY CARAMEL ICING

¼ pound (1 stick) butter or margarine, softened at room temperature
¼ cup firmly packed dark brown sugar
⅓ cup milk
1 teaspoon vanilla extract
1 (16 oz.) box confectioners' sugar

Preheat the oven to 350 degrees F. Grease and lightly flour the bottom of a 9x13x2-inch baking pan.

Combine the butter, sugar, and vanilla extract in a large mixing bowl. Beat until well blended. Add the eggs one at a time, beating well after each addition.

In a medium bowl, combine the flour, baking powder, salt, tea mix, cinnamon, nutmeg, and cloves. Stir to mix. Add to the batter alternately with the orange juice, starting and ending with the flour mixture. Pour into the prepared pan. Bake for about 25 minutes, or until a wooden pick inserted in the center of the cake comes out clean.

While the cake bakes, prepare the icing. In a medium saucepan, combine the butter, brown sugar, and milk. Bring to a boil. Remove from heat. Stir in the vanilla extract and confectioners' sugar. Beat until smooth.

Pour the caramel icing over the top of the cake while it is still warm. Allow to cool completely on a rack before slicing.

Holiday Fruit & Nut Cakes

········••••••••)) ⊛ (((•••••••········

FRUITCAKE

Yield: at least 20 servings

$\mathcal{M}$y mother always cut the candied fruit and nuts a day or two before she planned to make her fruitcake and she put a large container of them on top of the refrigerator. We all knew that they were there and would sneak in and grab a handful when Mother wasn't looking. Personally, I liked the candied cherries and pineapple best. To insure a moist cake, I place a pan of water on the rack beneath the one holding the cake pan.

2 cups chopped candied cherries
2 cups chopped candied pineapple
2 cups chopped dates (not the sugared kind)
1 cup chopped walnuts
1 cup chopped pecans
1½ cups raisins
2⅓ cups all-purpose flour
¾ teaspoon salt
1 teaspoon baking powder
1 teaspoon ground cinnamon
½ teaspoon grated nutmeg
½ teaspoon ground cloves
¼ pound (1 stick) butter or margarine, softened at room temperature
½ cup shortening
⅔ cup sugar
½ cup orange marmalade
5 eggs
½ cup grape juice

Preheat the oven to 250 degrees F. Grease a 10-inch tube pan. Cut a piece of wax paper to fit the bottom of the pan. Grease the paper. Flour the pan, shaking out any excess flour.

Combine the cherries, pineapple, dates, walnuts, pecans, and raisins in a large bowl. Sprinkle ⅓ cup of the flour over the fruit mixture and toss to coat. Set aside.

In a large bowl, combine the remaining 2 cups of flour, salt, baking powder, and spices. Stir to mix. In another large bowl, cream together the butter, shortening, sugar, and marmalade. Add the eggs one at a time, beating well after each addition. Add the flour mixture to the creamed mixture alternately with the juice. Mix well. Stir in the fruit mixture. Mix well.

Place a pan of water on the rack directly underneath the rack on which the cake pan will be placed. Pour the batter into the prepared tube pan. Bake for about 3½ hours, or until a wooden pick comes out clean when inserted near the center of the cake. Remove from the pan immediately. Wrap securely with aluminum foil or place in an airtight container. If desired, soak a large piece of cheesecloth in juice or liqueur and wrap around the cake.

NOTE: A liqueur can be substituted for the grape juice, if desired. Banana liqueur adds an interesting flavor.

Southern bakers usually make the traditional fruitcake at least a month before Christmas. It is wrapped in a thin white cloth or cheesecloth that is soaked in liquor, liqueur, or fruit juice and stored in an airtight container. My mother always placed thin slices of fresh apples over the cake before storing and would change the apples about every week. This insured an extra-moist fruitcake. The cake will keep for several weeks after Christmas if kept securely covered.

DATE PECAN CAKE

Yield: 20 servings

*W*hen I was growing up, Mother always made a date and pecan cake during the Christmas holidays. Her version was a compact cake with a texture similar to fruitcake. It was one of my favorites and I thought of it as a good substitute for fruitcake. I decided to see if I could develop a version that was lighter in texture yet tasted similar to the old-fashioned one. My date nut cake is indeed much lighter in texture, and the buttermilk glaze adds a bonus taste treat.

CAKE

½ pound (2 sticks) butter or margarine, softened at room temperature
1⅓ cups sugar
3 eggs
1 teaspoon vanilla extract
2 cups all-purpose flour
1 teaspoon baking soda
1 cup chopped pecans
1 cup chopped dates (not the sugared kind)
1 cup buttermilk

BUTTERMILK GLAZE

½ cup sugar
¼ cup buttermilk
¼ teaspoon baking soda
1½ teaspoons light corn syrup
2 tablespoons butter or margarine
½ teaspoon vanilla extract

Preheat the oven to 350 degrees F. Great a 10-inch tube pan. Line the bottom with wax paper cut to fit. Grease the paper and lightly flour the entire pan.

In a large bowl, combine the butter and sugar. Beat until well blended. Add the eggs one at a time, beating well after each addition. Add the vanilla. Mix well. In a medium bowl, combine the flour and baking soda. Stir to mix. Remove ¼ cup of the flour mixture and combine it in a small bowl with the pecans and dates. Toss lightly to coat the dates and pecans. Add the remaining flour to the creamed mixture alternately with the buttermilk. Mix well. Stir in the coated dates and pecans. Pour into the prepared pan. Reduce the oven temperature to 300 degrees F. Bake for 50 to 60 minutes, or until a wooden pick inserted near the center of the cake comes out clean. Cool in the pan for about 5 minutes. Turn out of pan onto a cake rack. Remove paper. Invert onto a cake plate.

Combine all glaze ingredients in a medium saucepan. Keep in mind that the baking soda will cause the mixture to foam, so you will need a pan deep enough to allow for this.

Bring the mixture to a boil. Reduce heat to medium-high. Cook for about 1 minute, stirring constantly. Remove from heat, cool for 5 minutes, and slowly pour over the warm cake.

CHRISTMAS CANDY CAKE

Yield: 15 to 18 servings

Fruitcakes have never been a favorite with me, but I remember my mother making one that I liked. It tasted like candy with lots of candied fruit and nuts in it. It also had graham crackers, but I chose to omit them from this recipe. Mother called her version "icebox fruitcake." A few years ago a friend gave me a recipe that reminded me of the one Mother made. I have combined what I can remember of my mother's cake with some of the ideas from my friend's cake. This is super rich and should be cut into small servings.

1⅓ cups chopped candied red cherries
1 cup chopped candied pineapple
1½ cups chopped dates (not the sugared kind)
1 tablespoon all-purpose flour
4½ cups chopped pecans or walnuts
1¼ cups coconut (canned or in plastic bags)
1 (14 oz.) can sweetened condensed milk

Preheat the oven to 250 degrees F. Grease and flour a 9-inch springform pan with tube insert.

Combine the cherries, pineapple, dates, and flour in a large bowl. Toss to coat the fruit with the flour. Add the pecans and coconut. Mix well. Add the condensed milk. Mix well.

Press into prepared pan and bake for 1½ hours. Cool completely before removing from pan. Wrap tightly in aluminum foil. It will keep, refrigerated, for several weeks.

Cake Roll-Ups

---······•◦◦◦◦•◦)●((◦◦•◦◦◦◦•·------

FRUIT NUT ROLL-UP

Yield: 10 servings

$\mathcal{T}$he filling for this sponge roll-up bakes right along with the cake. When it comes from the pan, you give it a roll and, like magic, you have your dessert ready to serve.

4 tablespoons butter
1 (8¼ oz.) can crushed pineapple, well drained (reserve the juice)
1 cup coconut (canned or in plastic bags)
1 cup chopped walnuts
1 (14 oz.) can sweetened condensed milk
¾ cup all-purpose flour
½ teaspoon ground cinnamon
½ teaspoon ground ginger
¼ teaspoon baking soda
¼ teaspoon salt
3 eggs
1 cup sugar
⅓ cup reserved pineapple juice
1 teaspoon vanilla extract
Confectioners' sugar
1 cup heavy cream, sweetened and whipped (optional)

Preheat the oven to 375 degrees F. Line a 10x15x1-inch jelly-roll pan with aluminum foil. Melt the butter in the pan and spread evenly.

Combine the drained pineapple, coconut, and walnuts in a medium bowl. Stir to mix. Spoon this mixture evenly in the pan. Drizzle the condensed milk over the fruit mixture.

(continued)

In a small bowl, combine the flour, cinnamon, ginger, baking soda, and salt. Stir to mix. In a large mixing bowl, beat the eggs for about 2 minutes, until light and fluffy. Add sugar. Beat until well blended. Add the flour mixture, pineapple juice, and vanilla. Beat until smooth. Pour into the pan. Bake for 20 to 25 minutes, until the cake springs back when lightly touched.

Remove from the oven. Sprinkle generously with the confectioners' sugar. Cover with a clean dish towel and invert. Remove the foil. Roll jelly-roll fashion, from the 10-inch side. Wrap the towel around the roll until cool. Sprinkle with more confectioners' sugar. Serve with whipped cream, if desired.

CHOCOLATE CHERRY ROLL-UP

Yield: 10 servings

A light and fluffy cherry pecan filling is spread over a delicate chocolate sponge cake and rolled up, making a delightful dessert for special guests.

CAKE
1 cup sifted all-purpose flour
3 tablespoons cocoa
1/4 teaspoon baking soda
1/8 teaspoon salt
3 eggs
1 cup sugar
1/3 cup amaretto liqueur
1 teaspoon vanilla extract
Confectioners' sugar

CHERRY PECAN FILLING
1/4 pound (1 stick) butter or margarine, softened at room temperature
1 teaspoon vanilla extract
2 tablespoons water
3 to 3 1/2 cups confectioners' sugar
1/2 cup chopped toasted pecans
1/2 cup chopped candied cherries

Preheat the oven to 350 degrees F. Line a 10x15x1-inch jelly roll pan with aluminum foil. Grease well.

In a small bowl, combine the flour, cocoa, baking soda, and salt. Stir to mix.

Beat the eggs in a large mixing bowl for about 2 minutes, until the eggs are light and fluffy. Add the sugar to the eggs. Beat well. Add the flour mixture alternately with the amaretto liqueur. Add the vanilla. Mix until blended. Pour the batter into the prepared pan. Bake for 15 to 20 minutes, until the cake springs back when lightly touched. Remove from the oven and sprinkle generously with confectioners' sugar. Cover with a clean dish towel and invert. Remove the foil. Roll the cake jelly-roll fashion, from the 10-inch side. Roll the towel in with the cake.

To make the filling, combine the butter, vanilla extract, water, and confectioners' sugar in a large mixing bowl. Beat until light and fluffy. If the consistency is too thick, add a little more water. If it doesn't seem to be thick enough to spread smoothly, add more confectioner's sugar. Stir in the pecans and cherries.

When the cake is completely cooled, unroll it and spread with the cherry pecan filling. Roll back up, starting again from the 10-inch side. Cut into slices about 1-inch thick.

Pound (and Bundt) Cakes

OLD-FASHIONED POUND CAKE

Yield: 20 servings

This is one of my favorite pound cake recipes. I found it in a large box of unfiled recipes. I don't know when or where I got the recipe, but I could tell from the handwriting that it was probably written by an elderly person. I have updated it by substituting exact measurements for the "pinch" and the "sprinkle." This recipe makes a big cake so be sure you use a large tube pan. Lining the bottom of the pan with wax paper helps to remove the cake.

12 tablespoons (1½ sticks) butter, softened at room temperature
¾ cup shortening
2¾ cups sugar
5 eggs
3 cups all-purpose flour
½ teaspoon baking powder
⅛ teaspoon salt
1 cup milk
1 teaspoon vanilla extract

Preheat the oven to 350 degrees F. Grease and flour a 10-inch tube pan. Line the bottom with wax paper, grease the paper and lightly dust it with flour.

Combine the butter, shortening, and sugar in a large bowl. Beat until creamy. Add the eggs one at a time, beating well after each addition.

In a medium bowl, combine the flour, baking powder, and salt. Stir to mix. Add the flour mixture to the creamed mixture alternately with the milk, starting and ending with the flour. Add the vanilla. Mix well. Pour the batter into the prepared pan. Bake for 1 hour and 10 minutes, or until a wooden pick comes out clean when inserted into the center of the cake. Allow to cool in the pan for about 10 minutes before turning the cake onto a cake plate.

COCONUT CREAM POUND CAKE

Yield: 18 to 20 servings

*T*his is an easy cake to make and its wonderful texture and flavor will make you want to bake it over and over again for friends and family. I made a similar cake many years ago using a cake mix, but this one made from scratch is much better. The ease of preparation makes this a good Busy Baker cake.

3 cups all-purpose flour
2 teaspoons baking powder
¼ teaspoon salt
½ cup shortening
12 tablespoons (1½ sticks) butter or margarine, softened at room
    temperature
2 whole eggs
3 egg whites
1½ teaspoons coconut extract
1 cup heavy cream
1 (6 oz.) package (about 1½ cups) frozen coconut

Preheat the oven to 350 degrees F. Grease and lightly flour a 10-inch tube or Bundt pan.

Combine the flour, baking powder, and salt in a large mixing bowl and stir to mix. Add the shortening, butter, whole eggs, egg whites, coconut extract, cream, and coconut. Beat with a mixer on low speed for about 1 minute, and then on medium-high speed for 2 minutes. The batter will be thick and fluffy. Spoon into the prepared pan. Bake for 1 hour, or until a wooden pick comes out clean when inserted near the center of the cake. As soon as the cake comes from the oven, turn it out of the pan onto a cake plate. Allow to cool before slicing.

SOUR CREAM POUND CAKE

Yield: 20 servings

I remember the first time I tasted sour cream pound cake. The thing that amazed me about this cake was its smooth texture and wonderful taste.

¼ *pound (1 stick) butter or margarine, softened at room temperature*
½ *cup shortening*
3 cups sugar
6 eggs
3 cups all-purpose flour
¼ *teaspoon baking soda*
¼ *teaspoon salt*
1 cup sour cream
2 teaspoons vanilla extract

Preheat the oven to 325 degrees F. Grease and lightly flour a 10-inch tube or Bundt pan.

In a large bowl, cream together the butter, shortening, and sugar. Add the eggs one at a time, beating well after each addition. This step is important because the eggs supply most of the leavening for the cake.

In a medium bowl, combine the flour, baking soda, and salt. Stir to mix. Add to the creamed mixture alternately with the sour cream, starting and ending with the flour. Add the vanilla and blend well. Pour into the prepared pan and bake for 1½ hours, or until a wooden pick comes out clean when inserted near the center of the cake. Cool in the pan for about 10 minutes. Invert onto a serving plate.

AMBROSIA POUND CAKE

Yield: about 20 servings

*W*hen the family gathered at my parents' home for Christmas dinner, the meal was never complete until we had enjoyed a bowl of ambrosia. The basic ingredients for ambrosia are coconut, oranges, and sugar, but Mother sometimes added other fruits. This moist cake captures that wonderful ambrosia flavor.

12 tablespoons (1½ sticks) butter or margarine, softened at room
    temperature
¾ cup shortening
2½ cups sugar
5 eggs
2 teaspoons coconut extract
3 cups all-purpose flour
½ teaspoon baking soda
¼ teaspoon salt
1 cup freshly squeezed orange juice
1 cup coconut (canned or in plastic bags)

Grease and flour a 10-inch tube or Bundt pan. In a large mixing bowl, combine the butter, shortening, and sugar. Beat until well blended. Add the eggs one at a time, beating well after each addition. Add the coconut extract and mix well.

In a medium bowl, combine the flour, baking soda, and salt. Stir to mix. Add to the batter alternately with the orange juice, starting and ending with the flour mixture. Stir in the coconut. Pour into the prepared pan. Place the pan in a *cold* oven. Set the temperature at 325 degrees F. Bake for 1 hour and 25 minutes, or until a wooden pick comes out clean when inserted near the center of the cake. Turn out of the pan immediately.

SUNSHINE POUND CAKE

Yield: about 20 servings

A bite of this cake is like a ray of sunshine for the palate. It has a beautiful smooth texture and a light citrus flavor.

½ pound (2 sticks) butter, softened at room temperature
⅓ cup shortening
8 ounces cream cheese, softened at room temperature
2¾ cups sugar
5 large eggs
3 cups all-purpose flour
¼ cup freshly squeezed orange juice
1 tablespoon pure lemon extract

Preheat the oven to 325 degrees F. Grease and lightly flour a 10-inch tube pan. Line the bottom of the pan with a circle of wax paper. Grease the paper and lightly dust with flour.

In a large mixing bowl, cream together the butter, shortening, and cream cheese. Add the sugar. Beat until smooth. Add the eggs one at a time, beating well after each addition. This is an important step because the eggs add the leavening to this cake. Add the flour alternately with the orange juice. Add the lemon extract. Mix well. Pour the batter into the prepared pan. Bake for about 1 hour 15 minutes, or until a wooden pick comes out clean when inserted near the center of the cake. Allow the cake to cool for about 10 minutes before removing it from the pan.

MOCHA NUT POUND CAKE

Yield: about 20 servings

*R*ecipe ideas sometimes come to me in unusual ways. This cake was named before it was developed. One day I was reading my favorite recipe for coconut pound cake and the words "mocha nut" came to mind. Perhaps it was because it rhymes with coconut. Anyway, it seemed like a good idea for a new pound cake. I had some coffee left over from breakfast so I decided to pursue this idea. It turned out great! Chocolate and coffee make a winning flavor combo whether it's ice cream or cake.

½ pound (2 sticks) butter or margarine, softened at room temperature
½ cup shortening
1¾ cups sugar
¾ cup firmly packed light brown sugar
5 eggs
1½ teaspoons vanilla extract
3 cups all-purpose flour
½ teaspoon baking soda
¼ teaspoon salt
¼ cup cocoa
¾ cup buttermilk
¼ cup strong coffee
1½ cups chopped walnuts

Preheat the oven to 350 degrees F. Grease and lightly flour a 10-inch tube or Bundt pan.

Cream together the butter, shortening, sugar, and brown sugar. Add the eggs one at a time, beating well after each addition. This is an important step because the eggs add most of the leavening in this cake. Add the vanilla. Beat well.

Combine the flour, baking soda, salt, and cocoa in a large bowl. Stir to mix. Combine the buttermilk and coffee. Add the flour mixture to the creamed mixture alternately with the buttermilk and coffee. Beat well. Stir in the walnuts. Pour into the prepared pan. Bake for about 1 hour, or until a wooden pick comes out clean when inserted near the center of the cake. Turn out of the pan immediately.

"FULL OF FRECKLES"
POUND CAKE

....

Yield: about 20 servings

This unusual name just seems to fit the cake. Miniature chocolate chips form the "freckles" in this light and luscious cream cheese pound cake. I got the idea for making this cake after tasting a delicious cheesecake made with the mini-chips.

¾ pound (3 sticks) butter or margarine, softened at room temperature
8 ounces cream cheese, softened at room temperature
3 cups sugar
5 eggs
3 cups all-purpose flour
¼ cup milk
1½ cups miniature chocolate chips

Preheat the oven to 325 degrees F. Grease and flour a 10-inch tube pan.

Combine the butter and cream cheese in a large mixing bowl. Beat until well blended. Add the sugar and beat until smooth and creamy. Add the eggs one at a time, beating well after each addition. This is an important step because the eggs add the leavening to the cake. Add the flour alternately with the milk, starting and ending with the flour. Stir in the mini-chips.

Pour into the prepared pan and bake for about 1½ hours, or until a wooden pick comes out clean when inserted near the center of the cake. Remove from the pan immediately and turn upright onto a serving plate. Allow to cool before slicing.

Strawberry Twist Coffeecake (page 238), and *left*, Fresh Coconut Cake (page 12).

Old-Fashioned Syrup Cake
(page 80), and *below*, Berry Patch
Cobbler Roll (page 173).

Beer Cheese Bread,
above (page 224), and
Pepper Casserole
Bread (page 228).

From top, clockwise: Almond Cherry Macaroons (page 96), Chocolate Munchies (page 103), Pumpkin Chippers (page 100), and Jiffy Spritz (page 129).

Clockwise from bottom left: Easy Cobbler (page 196), Black Walnut Cake (page 30), and Fruit Nut Roll-Up (page 55).

Japanese Fruitcake Squares (page 40), and *below*, Chocolate Cream Pie in Peanut Butter Crust (page 142).

Clockwise from above: Old-Fashioned Apple Pie (page 158), Mama's Lane Cake (page 34), Southern Biscuits (page 205).

Sweet Potato Pie (page 166).

Twist o'Lemon Bread Pudding (page 181).

RUM AND COLA COCO-CAKE

Yield: 18 to 20 servings

*R*um and Coca-Cola add an intense flavor to this chocolate cake. One taste tester remarked that this is a "chocoholic's delight"! This is the perfect partner for a dish of vanilla ice cream.

¾ pound (3 sticks) butter or margarine, softened at room temperature
2½ cups sugar
5 eggs
3 cups all-purpose flour
⅓ cup cocoa
½ teaspoon baking soda
⅛ teaspoon salt
½ cup buttermilk
½ cup Coca-Cola
3 tablespoons dark rum, or 1½ teaspoons rum extract
1 cup chopped walnuts

Preheat the oven to 350 degrees F. Grease and lightly flour a 12-cup Bundt pan or a 10-inch tube pan.

In a large mixing bowl, cream together the butter and sugar. Add the eggs one at a time, beating well after each addition.

Combine the flour, cocoa, baking soda, and salt in a medium bowl and stir to mix. Add to the creamed mixture alternately with the buttermilk and Coca-Cola. Add the rum and mix well. Stir in the walnuts. Pour into the prepared pan. Bake for 50 to 60 minutes, or until a wooden pick inserted near the center of the cake comes out clean. Remove from the pan immediately.

CHOCOLATE BUTTERMILK
POUND CAKE

Yield: about 20 servings

*T*his cake's delicate chocolate flavor and featherlike texture is sure to bring cheers from dessert lovers.

½ pound (2 sticks) butter or margarine, softened at room temperature
½ cup shortening
2½ cups sugar
5 eggs
3 cups all-purpose flour
½ teaspoon baking soda
¼ teaspoon salt
⅓ cup cocoa
1 cup buttermilk
1 teaspoon vanilla extract
1 cup finely chopped walnuts

Preheat the oven to 350 degrees F. Grease and flour a 10-inch tube pan.

In a large bowl, cream together the butter, shortening, and sugar. Add the eggs one at a time, beating well after each addition.

In a medium bowl, combine the flour, baking soda, salt, and cocoa. Stir to mix. Add to the creamed mixture alternately with the buttermilk, starting and ending with the flour mixture. Add the vanilla. Mix well. Stir in the walnuts. Pour into a prepared pan.

Bake for about 1 hour 10 minutes, or until a wooden pick comes out clean when inserted near the center of the cake. Immediately invert the cake onto a cake plate. Cool slightly before slicing.

APPLESAUCE CAKE

Yield: about 20 servings

*T*his old-fashioned cake is extra moist due to the applesauce, and it is delicately flavored with just a hint of cinnamon.

1 cup raisins
1 cup walnuts
2 cups unsweetened applesauce
¼ pound (1 stick) butter or margarine, softened at room temperature
½ cup shortening
2 cups sugar
3 eggs
1 teaspoon vanilla extract
3 cups all-purpose flour
1 teaspoon ground cinnamon
1½ teaspoons baking soda
¼ teaspoon salt

Preheat the oven to 350 degrees F. Grease and lightly flour a 10-inch tube or Bundt pan.

Combine the raisins and walnuts in the bowl of a food processor fitted with the steel blade. Process until the raisins and nuts are finely chopped, but not powdery. Combine the raisin-nut mixture with the applesauce in a medium bowl.

In a large mixing bowl, cream together the butter, shortening, and sugar. Add the eggs one at a time, beating well after each addition. Add the vanilla. Mix well.

Combine the flour, cinnamon, baking soda, and salt. Stir to mix. Add the flour mixture to the creamed mixture alternately with the applesauce mixture. Mix well. Spoon into the prepared pan and smooth the top. Bake for about 1 hour, or until a wooden pick comes out clean when inserted into the center of the cake. Remove from the pan immediately. Cool slightly before slicing.

NOTE: This cake is best served slightly warm, but it is also good completely cool. It also keeps well. It is extra moist and can be kept in a cake saver or wrapped in foil or plastic for at least two weeks. It also freezes well.

BANANA STREUSEL CAKE

Yield: about 16 servings

*B*ananas add a delicate flavor to this easy tube cake. The coconut pecan streusel adds the finishing touch. Several years ago a similar cake won the National Pillsbury Bake-Off. The streusel for that cake was made using a boxed frosting mix. Recently when I wanted to make the cake, I could not find any of the frosting mix in the supermarket. When I contacted the Pillsbury Company, I was told that Pillsbury no longer markets the frosting and that they had not modified the recipe so that it could be duplicated. I decided to try to modify it myself and was very pleased with my new version. Rum extract adds a new flavor accent.

STREUSEL

1 cup firmly packed dark brown sugar
⅓ cup all-purpose flour
⅓ cup quick-cooking oats (not instant)
1 cup chopped pecans
⅔ cup flaked coconut
6 tablespoons butter or margarine, melted

CAKE

4 eggs
1 cup sour cream
1½ cups thinly sliced ripe bananas
1 teaspoon rum extract
1 (18.25 oz.) box yellow cake mix

In a medium bowl, combine all the streusel ingredients except the melted butter. Mix well. Add the butter. Mix until crumbly. Set aside.

Preheat the oven to 350 degrees F. Grease and lightly flour a 10-inch tube pan.

Combine the eggs, sour cream, bananas, and rum extract in a large mixing bowl. Beat with an electric mixer until smooth. Add the cake mix. Beat for about 2 minutes, or until well mixed. Pour about 2 cups of the batter into the prepared pan. Sprinkle one third of the streusel over the batter. Repeat twice with batter and streusel.

Bake for about 55 minutes, or until a wooden pick inserted near the center of the cake comes out clean. Cool upright in pan for about 10 minutes. Turn out of the pan and invert onto a cake plate so that the crumb mixture will be on top.

BROWN SUGAR APPLE CAKE

Yield: about 20 servings

*A*pple cakes have been a favorite in the South for many years. Perhaps this is because apples are so plentiful. Brown sugar adds that special caramel flavor to this moist and light tube cake.

CAKE

¾ cup shortening
12 tablespoons (1½ sticks) butter or margarine, softened at room temperature
2 cups firmly packed light brown sugar
4 eggs
3 cups all-purpose flour
1 teaspoon baking soda
1 teaspoon ground cinnamon
¼ teaspoon salt
1 cup sour cream
2 cups peeled and chopped apples (red Delicious are good for this cake)

CARAMEL GLAZE

1 tablespoon butter or margarine, melted
2 tablespoons light brown sugar
2 tablespoons sour cream
¾ cup confectioners' sugar

Preheat the oven to 350 degrees F. Generously grease and lightly flour a 10-inch tube or Bundt pan.

In a large bowl, cream together the shortening, butter, and brown sugar. Add the eggs one at a time, beating well after each addition. *(continued)*

In a medium bowl, combine the flour, baking soda, cinnamon, and salt. Stir to mix. Add to the creamed mixture alternately with the sour cream, starting and ending with the flour. Stir in the apples. Pour into the prepared pan. Bake for about 1 hour, or until a wooden pick comes out clean when inserted near the center of the cake. Cool for about 10 minutes before removing from the pan. Invert onto a cake plate.

To make the glaze, combine the melted butter, brown sugar, and sour cream in a small bowl. Mix well. Gradually add the confectioners' sugar, beating until smooth. Drizzle over cake.

APPLE BLOSSOM CAKE

Yield: about 20 servings

*T*here are many versions of apple cake using a variety of different spices. My choice is simply cinnamon, and just a little of that. Spices should not be the dominant flavor in an apple cake. They should just enhance the flavor and you should be able to taste the apples. Brown sugar gives this moist cake a caramel taste. Almost any kind of apple will do for this cake. The first time I made it, the only apples I had on hand were two red Delicious and one Granny Smith. I combined the two and the cake turned out great.

CAKE
3 eggs
1⅓ cups vegetable oil
2 cups firmly packed light brown sugar
3 cups all-purpose flour
1 teaspoon baking soda
¼ teaspoon salt
1 teaspoon ground cinnamon
¾ cup chopped almonds
½ cup raisins
3 cups peeled, cored, and cubed apples (about 3 apples)

CARAMEL GLAZE

1 tablespoon butter or margarine
2 tablespoons firmly packed light brown sugar
2 tablespoons milk
⅔ cup confectioners' sugar
2 tablespoons sliced almonds (optional)

Preheat the oven to 350 degrees F. Generously grease and lightly flour a 10-inch tube or Bundt pan.

Combine the eggs, oil, and brown sugar in a large mixing bowl. Beat until well blended. Combine the flour, baking soda, salt, and cinnamon in a medium bowl. Stir to mix. Gradually add to the egg mixture. Mix well. Stir in the almonds, raisins, and apples. Pour into the prepared pan. Bake for about 1 hour, or until a wooden pick comes out clean when inserted near the center of the cake. Turn out of the pan immediately. Allow to cool slightly.

To make the glaze, melt the butter in a small saucepan or in a microwave. Stir in the brown sugar and milk. Mix until blended. Add the confectioners' sugar and beat until smooth. Spoon over top of cake and allow to drip down the sides. Sprinkle almonds on top of the cake.

Other Cakes

--------∙∙∙◦◦◦◦◦◦◦D◈C◦◦◦◦◦◦◦◦∙∙∙--------

COCONUT LEMONADE LOAF

Yield: about 10 servings

*F*rozen lemonade concentrate gives this loaf a tangy zing. The baking pan is generously coated with coconut cookie crumbs, which add flavor and a crisp texture to the outside of the loaf.

LOAF

¼ cup finely ground coconut cookie crumbs
5½ tablespoons butter or margarine, melted
1 cup sugar
2 eggs
1½ cups all-purpose flour
1 teaspoon baking powder
¼ teaspoon salt
½ cup milk
1 tablespoon undiluted lemonade concentrate
½ cup finely chopped pecans

LEMONADE GLAZE

½ cup undiluted lemonade concentrate
½ cup sugar
¼ teaspoon coconut flavoring

Preheat the oven to 350 degrees F. Generously grease a 9x5x3-inch loaf pan. Coat the pan with the cookie crumbs, shaking out any excess.

In a large bowl, beat together the butter, sugar, and eggs. In a medium bowl, combine the flour, baking powder, and salt. Stir to mix. Add to the creamed mixture alternately with the milk, starting and ending with the flour mixture. Add the lemonade concentrate. Mix well. Stir in the pecans. Pour the batter into the prepared loaf pan. Bake for 40 to 45 minutes, or until a wooden pick comes out clean when inserted into the center of the loaf.

While the loaf is baking, make the glaze. Combine the lemonade with the sugar in a small saucepan. Cook over medium heat until the sugar dissolves. Add the coconut flavoring. Remove from the heat.

As soon as the cake comes from the oven, slowly spoon the lemonade glaze over the cake, allowing it to seep into the cake. Cool in the pan. Remove from the pan and, when the loaf is completely cooled, wrap securely with plastic wrap. It is best not to cut the cake for about 24 hours because it gets better the longer you can wait. Securely wrapped, it will keep for a week.

NOTE: For serving as a finger sweet at a cocktail buffet, make miniature lemonade loaves using three (approximately 4½x2x2-inch) pans. Bake for about 30 minutes. Cut the loaves into thin slices.

FRIENDSHIP CUPCAKES

Yield: 15 cupcakes

Sometimes even simple recipes are special, and this one falls into that category. The texture is a little unusual for cupcakes because the tops get crispy, which really makes them better. One of our daughters said that the crisp top makes them taste like Southern tea cakes. Cupcakes were probably the first thing I ever learned to cook. One of our neighbors, originally from Detroit, had married a Southern "boy." Many times, while her husband was at night school, I would visit Frances and her small son. We would almost always make cupcakes similar to these and frost them with chocolate icing. We always enjoyed them with a big glass of icy cold milk while we listened to the radio. Why didn't we just watch TV? Simple. As strange as it might seem to today's youngsters, we didn't have TV back then. These are not soft and moist cupcakes like those from a cake mix, but they are indeed special.

5½ tablespoons butter or margarine, softened at room temperature
1 cup sugar
1 teaspoon vanilla extract
1 egg
2 cups all-purpose flour
1 teaspoon baking powder
⅔ cup milk

FUDGE FROSTING

1½ cups sugar
1 tablespoon cocoa
4 tablespoons butter or margarine
½ cup milk
1 teaspoon vanilla extract

Preheat the oven to 350 degrees F. Place paper liners in each of 15 muffin cups.

In a large bowl, combine the butter, sugar, vanilla, and egg. Beat until well blended. In a small bowl, combine the flour and baking powder. Stir to mix. Gradually add the flour mixture to the creamed mixture alternately with the milk, starting and ending with the flour. Fill the cupcake liners about two thirds full. Bake for about 25 minutes, or until a wooden pick comes out clean when inserted into the center of one of the cupcakes. Remove the cupcakes from the muffin tins and place on a rack to cool before frosting.

To make the frosting, combine the sugar, cocoa, butter, and milk in a medium saucepan. Cook over medium heat until mixture reaches the soft ball stage when a little is dropped into cold water. Stir in vanilla extract. Beat until smooth and thickened. Spread on top of cupcakes.

ORANGE MELTAWAYS

Yield: 6½ dozen miniature cakes

*T*hese miniature cakes are perfect for serving with afternoon tea or as an after-school snack with a glass of milk. This is an easy "from scratch" version of the melt-in-your-mouth cakelettes originally made from a cake mix. A dunking in an orange and lemon glaze gives these tiny cakes a zingy taste.

3 cups all-purpose flour
1 (2.9 oz.) package vanilla pudding mix (not instant)
1 tablespoon baking powder
¼ teaspoon salt
3 cups sugar
½ pound (2 sticks) butter or margarine, softened at room temperature
3 eggs
1 cup freshly squeezed orange juice
½ cup ice water

GLAZE
1 (16 oz.) box confectioners' sugar
½ cup freshly squeezed orange juice
¼ cup freshly squeezed lemon juice

Preheat the oven to 350 degrees F. Grease as many miniature muffin pans as are available. Most miniature muffin pans make a dozen small muffins and each muffin cup has a capacity of 2 tablespoons. *(continued)*

Combine the flour, pudding mix, baking powder, salt, and sugar in a large mixing bowl. Stir to mix. Add the butter, eggs, orange juice, and ice water. Using an electric mixer, beat on low speed for about 1 minute and then on high speed for about 2 minutes. Spoon into muffin tins, filling each miniature cup about two thirds full. Bake for 10 to 12 minutes, or until a wooden pick comes out clean when inserted into the center of one of the cakes.

While the cakes are baking, make the glaze by combining the confectioners' sugar, orange juice, and lemon juice in a medium bowl. Beat until smooth. This mixture will be thin. As soon as the cakes come from the oven, drop them into the glaze, coating well. As you take the cakes out of the glaze, place them on a rack (be sure that you have wax paper underneath the rack to catch the drippings). Allow the glaze to set before serving.

Busy Baker Cakes

BUTTER PECAN CAKE

Yield: 15 to 18 servings

*T*his simple-to-make sheet cake has a moist texture and a sensational flavor.

1⅓ cups milk
1 cup quick-cooking oats (not instant)
¼ cup (1 stick) butter or margarine, softened at room temperature
1 (3⅝ oz.) box butter pecan instant pudding mix (reserve ¼ cup for topping)
⅔ cup sugar
⅔ cup firmly packed light brown sugar
2 eggs
1½ cups all-purpose flour
1 teaspoon baking soda
½ teaspoon salt
1 teaspoon vanilla extract

TOPPING

¼ cup reserved pudding mix
½ cup firmly packed light brown sugar
½ cup sugar
4 tablespoons butter or margarine, softened at room temperature
1 teaspoon vanilla extract
¼ cup milk
½ cup chopped pecans
1 cup coconut (canned or in plastic bags)

Preheat the oven to 350 degrees F. Grease and lightly flour a 9x13x2-inch baking pan.

Heat the milk in a small saucepan. Do not let it boil. Remove from the heat immediately. Stir in the oats. Set aside.

Combine the butter, pudding mix (except the reserved ¼ cup), sugar, brown sugar, eggs, flour, baking soda, salt, and vanilla. Beat until well mixed. Add oat mixture. Beat until smooth. Pour into the prepared pan. Bake for 25 to 30 minutes, or until a wooden pick comes out clean when inserted into the center of the cake.

While the cake is baking, prepare the topping. Combine all the ingredients in a small mixing bowl. Mix well. As soon as the cake is done, spread immediately with the topping. Place under the broiler for about 3 minutes, or until lightly browned.

CORN BREAD CAKE

Yield: 12 servings

Don't let the name fool you. This delicious cake doesn't taste anything like corn bread and there's no cornmeal in it. I don't know how it got the name, but there's something about the way the cake looks when it comes from the oven that reminds you of corn bread. Once you take a bite, the thoughts of corn bread quickly vanish. This unadorned cake is so simple to make that you don't even need a mixer. It is so tasty that it doesn't need an icing. As the cake bakes it will rise and then fall a little due to the amount of sugar, which also gives the cake a slightly chewy texture.

4 eggs
2 cups firmly packed light brown sugar
1 cup oil
2 cups self-rising flour
1½ teaspoons butter-flavored extract
1 cup chopped pecans

Preheat the oven to 350 degrees F. Grease a 9x13x2-inch baking pan.

Break the eggs into a large mixing bowl and beat slightly with a fork. Add the remaining ingredients in order listed and mix well after each addition. Pour the batter into the prepared pan. Bake for about 45 minutes, or until a wooden pick comes out clean when inserted near the center of the cake. Cool in the pan on a rack.

OLD-FASHIONED SYRUP CAKE

Yield: about 15 servings

When someone in the South says, "Pass the syrup," they usually mean sorghum. As a child, I remember that every time our syrup supply got low, Daddy would drive about 40 miles to the syrup mill on Sand Mountain for a gallon bucket of sorghum. Sometimes we enjoyed it with butter and biscuits, but my favorite sorghum treat was one of Mother's special popcorn balls. Syrup cake is another very old Southern dessert. This moist cake is usually served plain, but it is also delicious with applesauce or just sprinkled with confectioners' sugar. Of course, you can also dress it up a bit with a little whipped cream. If you don't have any sorghum on hand, you can substitute unsulfured molasses.

> ½ cup firmly packed brown sugar
> ¼ pound (1 stick) butter or margarine, softened at room temperature
> 1 cup sorghum syrup
> 2 cups all-purpose flour
> 1 teaspoon baking soda
> ½ teaspoon salt
> 1 teaspoon ground cinnamon
> 1 cup hot water

Preheat the oven to 350 degrees F. Grease and lightly flour a 9x13x2-inch baking pan.

In a large bowl, cream together the brown sugar and butter. Add the syrup. Beat well. Combine the flour, baking soda, salt, and cinnamon in a medium bowl. Stir to mix. Add to the creamed mixture alternately with the hot water. Mix well. The batter will be thin. Pour into the prepared pan. Bake for 25 to 30 minutes, or until a wooden pick inserted near the center comes out clean. Best served slightly warm or at room temperature.

SOUR CREAM COCONUT CAKE

Yield: 15 to 18 servings

A cake similar to this one became popular several years ago. It was a stacked yellow cake made from a mix and topped with a sour cream and coconut topping. I wanted to make a more flavorful batter and eliminate the cake mix. My version is frosted in the baking pan.

CAKE
½ pound (2 sticks) butter or margarine, softened at room temperature
2 cups sugar
3 eggs
3½ cups all-purpose flour
1½ teaspoons baking soda
¼ teaspoon salt
1 cup buttermilk
1½ teaspoons coconut extract

SOUR CREAM COCONUT TOPPING
1 (12 oz.) package frozen coconut, thawed
1½ cups sugar
⅛ teaspoon salt
¾ cup sour cream

Preheat the oven to 350 degrees F. Grease and lightly flour the bottom of a 9x13x2-inch baking pan.

Combine all the cake ingredients in a large mixing bowl. Beat until smooth. Pour into prepared pan. Bake for about 30 minutes, or until a wooden pick comes out clean when inserted into the center of the cake.

While the cake is baking, combine all the topping ingredients in a medium bowl and mix well. As soon as the cake comes from the oven, punch several holes in the warm cake layer using a fork. Spread the topping evenly over the cake. Allow to cool before slicing.

QUICK-AND-EASY JAM CAKE

Yield: about 18 servings

*J*am cake has been a favorite in the South for many, many years, but few modern-day Southern bakers make the original version because it is time consuming. If you long for a taste of Mom's jam cake but don't have the time to make the old-fashioned kind, this simple version might help you to recapture that wonderful flavor that many of us remember from our youth. Although the ingredients list is long, the preparation method is quick and easy.

3 cups self-rising flour
¾ cup sugar
¾ cup firmly packed light brown sugar
¾ teaspoon ground cinnamon
⅛ teaspoon ground cloves
⅛ teaspoon grated nutmeg
1 cup seedless blackberry jam
1 cup sour cream
3 eggs
12 tablespoons (1½ sticks) butter or margarine, softened at room temperature
½ cup raisins
1 cup chopped pecans

EASY CARAMEL FROSTING
¼ pound (1 stick) butter or margarine
1 cup firmly packed dark brown sugar
1 (16 oz.) box confectioners' sugar
¼ cup milk

Preheat the oven to 350 degrees F. Grease and lightly flour the bottom of a 9x13x2-inch baking pan.

In a large mixing bowl, combine the flour, both sugars, spices, jam, sour cream, eggs, and butter. Mix well. Stir in the raisins and pecans. Pour into the cake pan. Bake for 40 to 45 minutes, or until a wooden pick comes out clean when inserted into the center of the cake. Cool the cake in the pan on a rack.

While the cake is cooling, prepare the frosting. Combine the butter and brown sugar in a small saucepan. Heat until the sugar is dissolved and the butter has melted. Pour into a large mixing bowl. Add the confectioners' sugar and milk. Beat until smooth. When the cake is completely cooled, spread the frosting evenly over the top.

NOTE: If the icing gets too thick, thin with a little more milk. If it fails to thicken enough, simply add more confectioners' sugar.

QUICK-AS-A-WINK
ICE CREAM CAKE

Yield: 15 to 20 servings

*T*his cake is so simple that anyone can make it. Another bonus is the variety of ways in which it can be served. A drizzle of glaze turns it into a breakfast treat. A scoop of vanilla ice cream or whipped cream turns it into an elegant dinner dessert. It is also good just sprinkled with confectioners' sugar. I developed the recipe about fifteen years ago and a postscript on the bottom of that old recipe describes the cake perfectly: "simplicity in disguise."

1 (15.4 oz.) box nut bread mix
1 cup vanilla ice cream
1 (8 oz.) can crushed pineapple, undrained
2 eggs
1 cup heavy cream, sweetened and whipped (optional)

Preheat the oven to 375 degrees F. Grease and lightly flour the bottom of a 9x13x2-inch baking pan.

Combine all ingredients except heavy cream. Beat 1 minute with an electric mixer. Pour into the prepared pan and bake for 20 to 22 minutes, or until a wooden pick comes out clean when inserted into the center of the cake. Allow to cool in the pan on a rack. Sprinkle with confectioners' sugar or serve with a scoop of ice cream or whipped cream.

UPSIDE-DOWN
GERMAN CHOCOLATE CAKE

Yield: about 20 servings

A creamy coconut and pecan frosting bakes underneath the feather-light chocolate layer. This is one of those after-work cakes that can be made quickly with little effort yet tastes as if you made it from scratch. It is rich so you will probably want to serve small slices.

1 (14 oz.) can sweetened condensed milk
½ cup chopped pecans
1 cup coconut (canned or in plastic bags)
1 (18.25 oz.) box German chocolate or milk chocolate cake mix
1 cup water
2 tablespoons sour cream
1 egg
2 egg whites
2 teaspoons coconut extract

Preheat the oven to 350 degrees F. Line a 9x13x2-inch baking pan with aluminum foil. Butter generously.

Combine the condensed milk, pecans, and coconut in a small bowl. Stir to mix. Pour into pan. Spread to cover bottom.

Combine the cake mix, water, sour cream, whole egg, egg whites, and coconut extract. Beat until well mixed, 2 to 3 minutes. Pour into pan. Bake for about 35 minutes, or until a wooden pick inserted near the center of the cake comes out clean. Remove from pan immediately. Remove foil. Allow to cool before slicing.

BLUEBERRY LEMON
MERINGUE CAKE

....

Yield: about 8 servings

*W*ith this recipe you can turn a simple box of blueberry muffin mix into a light and delicate cake with just a hint of lemon. It's topped with a nutty meringue that bakes along with the cake layer—easy but delicious. To fancy it up a bit, you can always add a dollop of whipped cream just before serving, but it also tastes great served plain.

3 eggs
1 (13 oz.) box blueberry muffin mix (one containing small wild blueberries is best)
½ cup sour cream
4 tablespoons sugar
2 teaspoons freshly squeezed lemon juice
¾ cup ground or very finely chopped walnuts

Preheat the oven to 350 degrees F. Grease and lightly flour the bottom only of a 7x11x1-inch baking pan (or a 9-inch square pan).

Separate 2 of the eggs. In a large mixing bowl, combine the muffin mix, sour cream, whole egg, 2 egg yolks, 2 tablespoons of the sugar, and the lemon juice. Beat until smooth. Fold in the drained blueberries. Pour into prepared pan.

In a small mixing bowl, beat the 2 egg whites until soft peaks form. Gradually add the remaining 2 tablespoons sugar. Beat only until the sugar is mixed into the whites. Fold in ground walnuts. The whites might deflate slightly with the addition of the nuts but that is okay. Spoon meringue over top of batter and spread to cover. Bake for 25 minutes, or until a wooden pick inserted in the center of the cake comes out clean.

Cookies

You can bring smiles to the faces of young and old alike by passing the cookie jar filled with such wonderful snacks as chocolate chip cookies, peanut butter cookies, sugar cookies, brownies, or oatmeal cookies with raisins. These have become classics. If you are in the South, you can add tea cakes to the list.

These much-loved cookies have seen some changes through the years but still remain among the most requested. Creative bakers add their own special touch to them.

If you don't have time to make a batch from scratch, try the exciting new Busy Baker cookies made from a box of pie crust mix. You will be surprised and delighted at the homemade quality of these super-easy cookies.

You will find that the cookies in this cookbook are easy to make and use only ingredients that most bakers keep on hand.

Remember that most of these recipes make several dozen cookies and you will need more than one cookie sheet. If you only have one, you must let the cookie sheet cool completely between each batch because the heat from the baking sheet will melt the cookie dough before it gets to the oven, and this can produce a less than satisfactory batch of cookies. If you are in a hurry, you can rinse the cookie sheet under cold water to hasten the cooling process.

Cookie Jar Favorites

Drop Cookies

OATMEAL COOKIES

Yield: 2½ to 3 dozen cookies

*W*hen I was growing up in a Southern home, the only flour I remember seeing in our kitchen was self-rising. You could almost always find a bag of self-rising soft wheat flour in the Southern pantry. Rather than buy "plain" flour (as all-purpose was called during those days), Mother would just use her self-rising to make cakes, cobblers, and cookies. These oatmeal cookies are made with self-rising flour, but you can substitute the same amount of all-purpose flour and add 1½ teaspoons of baking powder and ½ teaspoon salt.

1¼ cups self-rising flour
¼ teaspoon ground cinnamon
½ cup shortening
¾ cup firmly packed brown sugar
1 egg
1 teaspoon vanilla extract
1 cup quick-cooking oats (not instant)
½ cup raisins

Preheat the oven to 375 degrees F. Line as many cookie sheets as are available with aluminum foil.

In a large mixing bowl, combine the flour, cinnamon, shortening, brown sugar, egg, and vanilla extract. Beat until well mixed. Stir in the oats and raisins. Drop by teaspoonfuls onto foil-lined cookie sheets, spacing the cookies about 2 inches apart. Bake for 8 to 10 minutes, or until golden brown. Remove from pans immediately. Cool on a rack.

APPLE OATMEAL COOKIES

Yield: about 2½ dozen cookies

*T*hese delicious cookies are made with flavored instant oats. When you open the container in which they are stored, you get a delightful whiff of apple and cinnamon.

1¼ cups all-purpose flour
1 teaspoon baking powder
½ teaspoon ground cinnamon
⅛ teaspoon salt
¼ pound (1 stick) butter or margarine, softened at room temperature
¾ cup firmly packed light brown sugar
1 egg
½ teaspoon vanilla extract
½ cup apple and cinnamon instant oats
½ cup raisins

Preheat the oven to 350 degrees F. Line as many cookie sheets as are available with aluminum foil.

Combine the flour, baking powder, cinnamon, and salt. Stir to mix. Set aside. In a large bowl, cream together the butter and brown sugar. Add the egg and vanilla. Mix well. Gradually add the flour mixture, beating well. Stir in the oats and raisins. Drop from a teaspoon onto the cookie sheets, spacing the cookies about 2 inches apart. Bake for 12 to 15 minutes, until lightly browned. Remove from cookie sheets and place on a rack to cool before storing.

BANANA OATMEAL COOKIES

Yield: about 2½ dozen cookies

These semisoft cookies taste a lot like banana nut bread. They are the creation of my granddaughter, Meagan, and her friend, Julie. Meagan loves to cook and has been helping me in the kitchen since she was about 4 years old. One day after school the girls asked if they could bake something. We decided that it would be fun to see if we could come up with a tasty new cookie. In our search for ingredients, we found a small banana, oats, nuts, and other basic ingredients, which seemed to be a good start. We were all delighted when the cookies came from the oven and tasted just great!

¼ pound (1 stick) butter or margarine, softened at room temperature
1 cup firmly packed brown sugar
1 egg
1 teaspoon vanilla extract
¼ cup mashed banana
1¼ cups self-rising flour
½ teaspoon ground cinnamon
1¼ cups quick-cooking oats (not instant)
½ cup chopped pecans

Preheat the oven to 375 degrees F. Line as many cookie sheets as are available with aluminum foil.

In a large bowl, combine the butter, brown sugar, egg, vanilla, banana, flour, and cinnamon. Mix until well blended. Stir in the oats and pecans. Drop from a teaspoon onto foil-lined cookie sheets, spacing the cookies about 2 inches apart. Bake for 10 to 12 minutes, until golden brown. Remove from the cookie sheets and place on a rack to cool.

BLACK WALNUT
OATMEAL COOKIES

....

Yield: 6 dozen cookies

*W*hen you bite into one of these oatmeal delights, you almost think you are enjoying it with black walnut ice cream. The combination of black walnuts and vanilla chips gives the cookie that "ice cream" flavor.

½ pound (2 sticks) butter or margarine, softened at room temperature
¾ cup sugar
¾ cup firmly packed light brown sugar
2 eggs
1 teaspoon vanilla extract
2 cups self-rising flour
1 cup quick-cooking oats (not instant)
⅔ cup chopped black walnuts
½ cup vanilla-flavored chips

Preheat the oven to 350 degrees F. Line as many cookie sheets as are available with aluminum foil.

Combine the butter, both sugars, eggs, vanilla, and flour in a large bowl. Beat until blended. Stir in the oats, black walnuts, and vanilla chips.

Drop from a teaspoon onto the foil-lined cookie sheets, spacing the cookies about 2 inches apart. Bake for 12 to 14 minutes, until lightly browned. Remove from the cookie sheets immediately and cool on rack.

BENNE SEED COOKIES

Yield: about 6 dozen cookies

*B*enne seeds, also known as sesame seeds, were brought to America from Africa. They are a popular ingredient in Southern baking, especially in South Carolina. These cookies are very thin with a chewy crisp texture. In addition to using benne seeds in cookies, they are often used in an unsweetened cocktail wafer.

⅓ cup sesame seeds
¼ pound (1 stick) butter or margarine, softened at room temperature
1 cup firmly packed light brown sugar
1 egg
1 cup self-rising flour
1 teaspoon vanilla extract

Preheat the oven to 350 degrees F. Line as many cookie sheets as are available with aluminum foil.

Pour the sesame seeds into a shallow baking pan. Toast the seeds in the oven for about 10 minutes, stirring every 2 minutes to prevent burning. Remove from the oven and let cool before adding to cookie dough.

In a large mixing bowl, combine the butter, brown sugar, egg, flour, and vanilla. Beat until well mixed. Stir in toasted sesame seeds.

Drop the dough onto foil-lined sheets, using about ½ teaspoon for each cookie, and space the cookies at least 2 inches apart. Bake for 8 to 10 minutes, or until cookies are lightly browned. Remove from cookie sheets immediately and cool on racks.

ALMOND CHERRY MACAROONS

Yield: about 3 dozen macaroons

Macaroons are best when made with special "macaroon" coconut, which is extra fine and unsweetened. However, if macaroon coconut is not available, you can use the canned coconut that you find in supermarkets. When using the supermarket coconut, I give it a quick chopping in the food processor to make the texture finer. If the macaroon mixture seems too thin to drop from a teaspoon onto cookie sheets, add more coconut.

¼ cup water
1 teaspoon light corn syrup
1¼ cups sugar
3 cups coconut (canned or in plastic bags)
1 cup chopped almonds
½ cup chopped, well-drained maraschino cherries
4 egg whites

Preheat the oven to 325 degrees F. Lightly grease as many baking sheets as are available or line them with parchment paper.

Combine the water, corn syrup, and sugar in a medium saucepan. Bring to a boil. Reduce heat to medium. Cook until sugar dissolves. Remove from the heat. Cool slightly. Stir in the coconut, almonds, and cherries. Mix well. Stir in the unbeaten egg whites. Drop from a teaspoon onto prepared baking sheets. Bake for 20 to 25 minutes, or until the macaroons begin to brown around the edges. Remove from the cookie sheets immediately. Cool on a rack.

TRIPLE CHIP DELIGHTS

Yield: about 4 dozen cookies

A combination of semisweet chocolate chips, vanilla chips, and peanut butter chips gives this crisp cookie its superb flavor. A food processor is needed for this recipe because the chocolate chips are processed with the flour to make a chocolate-flavored flour. The vanilla and peanut butter chips are left whole to give the cookie a flavorful crunch.

2 cups all-purpose flour
1 cup semisweet chocolate chips
1 teaspoon baking soda
1⅓ cups sugar
12 tablespoons (1½ sticks) butter or margarine, softened at room
    temperature
2 eggs
1 cup vanilla chips
1 cup peanut butter chips
½ cup chopped pecans

Preheat the oven to 350 degrees F. Line as many cookie sheets as are available with aluminum foil.

Combine the flour, chocolate chips, and baking soda in the bowl of a food processor fitted with the steel blade. Process until the chips are as fine as the flour. Pour into a large mixing bowl. Add sugar, butter, and eggs. Beat until well mixed. Stir in vanilla chips, peanut butter chips, and pecans. Drop from a tablespoon onto the foil-lined cookie sheets, spacing the cookies at least 2 inches apart. Bake for 12 to 14 minutes. Cookies will be lightly browned. Remove from cookie sheets immediately. Cool on a rack.

DOUBLE CHOCOLATE
WALNUT DROPS

....

Yield: about 6 dozen cookies

*T*he depth of flavor in these crispy yet chewy cookies will be appreciated by chocolate lovers. Both cocoa and chocolate chips add a special fudgy flavor. That first bite will probably make you think you are enjoying a brownie with a slight crisp texture on the outside.

½ pound (2 sticks) butter or margarine, softened at room temperature
1 cup sugar
1 cup firmly packed light brown sugar
2 eggs
2¼ cups all-purpose flour
3 tablespoons cocoa
1 teaspoon baking soda
¼ teaspoon salt
1 cup coarsely chopped walnuts
1 cup chocolate chips
1 cup quick-cooking oats (not instant)

Preheat the oven to 375 degrees F. Line as many cookie sheets as are available with aluminum foil.

Combine the butter, sugar, and brown sugar in a large mixing bowl. Beat until well blended. Add eggs. Beat well. In a medium bowl, combine the flour, cocoa, baking soda, and salt. Stir to mix. Gradually add the flour mixture to the creamed mixture, beating well. Stir in walnuts, chocolate chips, and oats. Mix well. Drop from a teaspoon onto the foil-lined cookie sheets. Bake for 7 to 8 minutes, or until slightly darker around edges. Remove from cookie sheets immediately. Cool on a rack before storing.

Choco-Chunk
Peanut Butter Drops

Yield: about 5 dozen cookies

*T*hese cookies were developed after tasting a simple candy made with white chocolate and peanut butter crunch cereal. The candy was served at a wedding reception and the guests took home a taste that would stay on the palate long after the party was over. I decided to try to capture this tasty duo in a cookie. During baking, these cookies will puff, but as they cool they become thin. They are crisp on the outside, moist and chewy on the inside.

12 tablespoons (1½ sticks) butter or margarine, softened at room
    temperature
½ cup peanut butter
1 cup sugar
1 cup firmly packed light brown sugar
2 eggs
1½ teaspoons vanilla extract
2¼ cups all-purpose flour
1 teaspoon baking soda
¼ teaspoon salt
1¾ cups white chocolate chunks (cut a little larger than standard chips)

Preheat the oven to 350 degrees F.

Combine the butter, peanut butter, sugar, and brown sugar. Beat until blended. Add the eggs and vanilla extract. Beat well. Combine the flour, baking soda, and salt in a medium bowl. Stir to mix. Add to the creamed mixture gradually, beating well. Stir in the white chocolate chunks. Drop by rounded teaspoonfuls onto as many ungreased cookie sheets as are available. Bake for 10 to 12 minutes, until lightly browned. Remove from the cookie sheets immediately and cool on a rack.

NOTE: These can be made with vanilla chips but you won't get the same flavor as you do using white chocolate.

PUMPKIN CHIPPERS

Yield: about 5 dozen cookies

These cookies were developed especially for those who usually don't like pumpkin. The mashed pumpkin is mixed with a butterscotch-flavored mixture and almost every bite rewards you with a chunk of white chocolate or a crunchy nut. One pumpkin-hater said, "There's not a better cookie than this!" while another remarked, "Those little elves will have to work hard to top this!" Mission accomplished! You will need a food processor or a blender to make these.

> 2 cups all-purpose flour
> 1 cup butterscotch morsels
> 1 teaspoon baking soda
> 12 tablespoons butter or margarine (1½ sticks), softened at room
>   temperature
> ⅔ cup sugar
> ⅔ cup firmly packed brown sugar
> 1 egg
> ½ cup cooked, mashed pumpkin (or use canned pumpkin purée)
> 1 cup quick-cooking oats (not instant)
> 1 cup white chocolate chunks (cut from a bar of white chocolate)
> ⅔ cup chopped walnuts

Preheat the oven to 350 degrees F. Line as many cookie sheets as are available with aluminum foil.

In the bowl of a food processor fitted with the steel blade, combine the flour and butterscotch morsels. Process until the morsels are as fine as the flour. Pour into a large bowl. Add the baking soda, butter, sugar, brown sugar, egg, and pumpkin. Beat until well mixed. Stir in the oats, white chocolate, and walnuts. Drop from a teaspoon onto foil-lined cookie sheets, spacing the cookies about 2 inches apart. Bake for 12 to 14 minutes, until golden brown. Remove from the cookie sheets and cool completely on a rack. Store in an airtight container.

CHOCOLATE DROP COOKIES

Yield: about 6 dozen cookies

This is an old recipe that I have changed by using milk chocolate morsels instead of the semisweet blocks of chocolate. I found the original recipe tucked away in an old file and it was written in a childlike manner with chocolate spelled "chocklate," so I can only assume that one of our daughters tasted the cookies somewhere, liked them, and scribbled down the recipe. After a few revisions, I tried the recipe and can see why she liked it so much.

½ pound (2 sticks) butter or margarine, softened at room temperature
1 cup sugar
3 ounces milk chocolate morsels, melted
1 teaspoon vanilla extract
2 eggs
2½ cups all-purpose flour
½ teaspoon baking soda
⅛ teaspoon salt
1 cup chopped walnuts

Preheat the oven to 350 degrees F. Line as many cookie sheets as are available with aluminum foil.

In a large bowl, cream together the butter and sugar. Add the melted chocolate and vanilla. Mix well. Add the eggs and beat until blended. Combine the flour, baking soda, and salt in a medium bowl. Stir to mix. Gradually add the flour mixture to the creamed mixture, beating well. Stir in the walnuts. Drop from a teaspoon onto the foil-lined cookie sheets, spacing the cookies about 2 inches apart. Bake for 12 to 14 minutes, until you can see just a little browning around the edges. Remove from the cookie sheets immediately and cool on a rack.

ORANGE DATE DROPS

Yield: About 5 dozen cookies

This is a variation of some cookies that I remember from my teen years. How lucky I was to be visiting a friend just at the time when her mother was baking these cookies! It didn't take but a bite or two for me to realize that I wanted the recipe. I bake the cookies now for my grandchildren and I hope that they, too, will remember this wonderful taste for many years to come.

¼ *pound (1 stick) butter or margarine, softened at room temperature*
½ *cup shortening*
1 *cup firmly packed light brown sugar*
2 *eggs*
½ *cup fresh orange juice*
1 *tablespoon grated orange peel*
1 *teaspoon vanilla extract*
2 *cups all-purpose flour*
½ *teaspoon salt*
1 *teaspoon baking soda*
2 *cups quick-cooking oats (not instant)*
½ *cup chopped dates*
½ *cup chopped walnuts*

Preheat the oven to 375 degrees F. Line as many cookie sheets as are available with aluminum foil.

Cream together the butter, shortening, and brown sugar. Add eggs and beat well. Add orange juice, peel, and vanilla. Mix well.

In a small bowl, combine the flour, salt, and baking soda. Stir to mix. Add to the creamed mixture, beating well. Stir in the oats, dates, and walnuts. Drop from a teaspoon onto cookie sheets, spacing the cookies about 2 inches apart. Bake for 8 to 10 minutes. Cool on a rack.

Shaped or Rolled Cookies

·············•◦◦◦◦◦◦◦◦◦◦ ◉ ◖◖◦◦◦◦◦◦◦◦◦◦·············

CHOCOLATE MUNCHIES

Yield: about 3 dozen cookies

*T*hese could possibly best be described as "brownie rounds" because they have the flavor of brownies but are shaped cookies rather than bars. Topped with coconut and candied cherry halves, these cookies look as good as they taste.

¼ pound (1 stick) butter or margarine, softened at room temperature
1 cup sugar
2 cups all-purpose flour
¼ teaspoon salt
½ teaspoon baking soda
3 tablespoons cocoa
2 eggs
1 cup coconut (canned or in plastic bags)
18 to 20 candied cherries, halved

In a large mixing bowl, combine the butter, sugar, flour, salt, baking soda, cocoa, and eggs. Beat until well mixed. Refrigerate for about 30 minutes.

Preheat the oven to 375 degrees F. Line as many cookie sheets as are available with aluminum foil.

Shape the chilled dough into balls about 1 inch in diameter. Dip the top of each ball in coconut. Place on cookie sheets, coconut side up. Space the cookies about 2 inches apart. Press a candied cherry half into the top of each cookie. Bake for 10 to 12 minutes. Remove from the cookie sheets immediately. Place on a rack to cool.

BLUE CHIP THUMBPRINTS

Yield: 2 dozen cookies

*T*he combination of blueberry preserves and vanilla chips makes these thumbprints special. The vanilla chips can usually be found next to chocolate chips in the supermarket.

¼ pound (1 stick) butter or margarine, softened at room temperature
⅓ cup sugar
1 egg yolk
1 cup all-purpose flour
⅔ cup vanilla chips
½ cup finely chopped almonds
12 teaspoons blueberry preserves

Preheat the oven to 325 degrees F. Line as many cookie sheets as are available with aluminum foil.

In a medium bowl, combine the softened butter, sugar, egg yolk, and flour. Mix until well blended. Stir in the vanilla chips. Shape into balls about 1 inch in diameter. Roll in the almonds. Place on the cookie sheets, spacing the balls about 2 inches apart. Push your thumb into center of each ball, flattening it slightly and making a small well in the center. Spoon about ½ teaspoon of the preserves into each well. Bake about 20 minutes, until lightly browned. Remove from the cookie sheets immediately and cool on a rack.

BUTTERSCOTCH PECAN WAFERS

Yield: about 10 dozen 1½-inch cookies

*T*he blend of flavors in this extra crisp cookie is remarkable. I think my brother-in-law described it best when he said, "It's like a burst of flavor when you bite into one of them." There is no need to prechop the nuts because they are ground in a food processor right along with the flour and butterscotch morsels. Even the unbaked dough tastes like a bite of caramel.

1¼ cups all-purpose flour
1 cup pecans
1 cup butterscotch morsels
¾ teaspoon baking soda
¼ teaspoon salt
4 tablespoons butter or margarine
1 tablespoon buttermilk
⅓ cup sugar
⅓ cup firmly packed brown sugar
1 egg

Combine the flour, pecans, butterscotch morsels, baking soda, and salt in the bowl of a food processor fitted with the steel blade. Process until the mixture is almost as fine as flour.

In a small saucepan, heat together the butter, buttermilk, sugar, and brown sugar until the butter has melted and the sugars have dissolved. Add this mixture and the egg to the flour mixture. Beat just until mixed. Chill for about 15 minutes, or until the dough is firm enough to roll into small balls.

Preheat the oven to 375 degrees F. Using about ½ teaspoon of the chilled dough per cookie, roll into a small ball about the size of a marble (about ¾ inch in diameter). Place on as many ungreased cookie sheets as are available or one that has been lined with aluminum foil. Space the balls about 2 inches apart on the cookie sheet. Bake for 7 or 8 minutes, until lightly browned. Remove to a rack and cool completely.

HIDEAWAY BUTTER BALLS

Yield: 40 to 45 cookies

I developed these surprise cookies about 20 years ago. I had been making traditional butter balls for many years and decided that it would be fun to hide something inside so that when the family took a bite, they would be treated to more than just a basic cookie. Chocolate-covered malted milk balls seemed to be a good choice because the crisp texture is similar to that of the cookie.

½ pound (2 sticks) butter or margarine, softened at room temperature
½ cup confectioners' sugar
1 teaspoon vanilla extract
2½ cups all-purpose flour
1 cup finely chopped pecans
40 to 45 chocolate-covered malted milk balls
Confectioners' sugar for coating

Preheat the oven to 350 degrees F.

Combine the butter, sugar, vanilla, and flour in a large bowl. Mix until well blended. This is a very stiff mixture. Stir in the pecans. Shape a scant tablespoonful of the dough around each piece of candy, forming a ball that is about 1¼ inches in diameter. Place on as many ungreased cookie sheets as are available, spacing the balls about an inch apart. Bake for 12 to 15 minutes, until the cookies begin to turn a light brown. Do not overbake. Remove from the cookie sheets and roll each cookie in confectioners' sugar. After the cookies have cooled slightly, coat again with confectioners' sugar.

COCONUT OATMEAL
JUMBO CRISPS

Yield: 15 to 18 large cookies

*T*hese old-fashioned cookies feature a new twist of lemon.

1¼ cups all-purpose flour
½ teaspoon baking powder
¼ teaspoon salt
¼ pound (1 stick) butter or margarine, softened at room temperature
⅓ cup sugar
⅓ cup firmly packed brown sugar
1 egg
1 teaspoon vanilla extract
½ teaspoon lemon extract
1 cup quick-cooking oats (not instant)
½ cup coconut (canned or in plastic bags)

Preheat the oven to 375 degrees F. Line as many cookie sheets as are available with aluminum foil.

In a large mixing bowl, combine the flour, baking powder, salt, butter, sugar, brown sugar, egg, and extracts. Mix until well blended. Stir in the oats and coconut. This mixture will be thick. Roll portions into large balls about the size of golf balls. Place on cookie sheets, spacing the balls about 3 inches apart. Flatten to about ¼ inch thick, using the bottom of a glass. If the dough sticks to the glass, dip the bottom of the glass in sugar before pressing the cookie. Bake for 10 to 12 minutes, until golden brown. Remove from the pans immediately and cool on a rack. Store in an airtight container.

SNOW CHIP CRISPIES

Yield: about 4½ dozen cookies

*T*his sugar-coated crisp cookie is a combination of two all-time favorites: sugared sand tarts and chocolate chip cookies. A micro-chip (chocolate, that is) supplies the tiny hint of chocolate in this delightful cookie. It tastes like the sand tart, but once in a while you get just a wee bite of chocolate.

2½ cups all-purpose flour
½ pound (2 sticks) butter or margarine, softened at room temperature
¼ teaspoon salt
1 cup confectioners' sugar
1½ teaspoons vanilla extract
½ cup sliced almonds
½ cup miniature chocolate chips
Confectioners' sugar for coating

Preheat the oven to 400 degrees F. Line as many cookie sheets as are available with aluminum foil or parchment paper.

Combine the flour, butter, salt, sugar, and vanilla extract in a large mixing bowl. Beat until the mixture clings together. Stir in the almonds and miniature chips. Shape into balls about 1 inch in diameter. Place the balls on the cookie sheets, spacing them about 2 inches apart. With the fingertips or the bottom of a glass, flatten the cookies to a thickness of about ¼ inch. Bake for 8 to 10 minutes, until the cookies begin to brown around the edges. Remove from the pans immediately and coat with confectioners' sugar. Cool on a rack. Coat again with the confectioners' sugar.

SUGAR COOKIES

Yield: about 3 dozen cookies

*S*ugar cookies are not just a Southern favorite. They have universal appeal and every section of our country seems to have its own favorite recipe. These Southern sugar cookies are similar to tea cakes in taste, but they are a little more crisp and a bit sweeter.

½ pound (2 sticks) butter or margarine, softened at room temperature
1½ cups sugar
2 eggs
1½ teaspoons vanilla extract
4 cups all-purpose flour
1 teaspoon baking powder
¼ teaspoon salt
¼ cup milk
Additional sugar for dipping and sprinkling on top

Preheat the oven to 375 degrees F.

In a large bowl, cream together the butter and sugar. Add the eggs and vanilla. Beat well. In a medium bowl, combine the flour, baking powder, and salt. Add to the creamed mixture alternately with the milk, starting and ending with the flour mixture. This will be a soft dough. Refrigerate for about 30 minutes.

Roll portions of the chilled dough about the size of a large walnut between the palms of your hands to form balls. Dip the top of each ball into sugar and place sugar side up on as many ungreased cookie sheets as are available, spacing the cookies about 3 inches apart. Flatten to a thickness of about ¼ inch using the bottom of a glass. If the glass sticks to the cookies, dip it in sugar and then press the dough. Bake for about 12 minutes, until lightly browned. As soon as the cookies come from the oven, sprinkle generously with sugar. Remove from cookie sheets and cool on a rack. Stir in an airtight container.

OLD-FASHIONED
SOUTHERN TEA CAKES

Yield: 36 large cookies

*T*ea cakes remain one of the most popular cookies in the South. This not-too-sweet treat holds many wonderful memories for me. My granny would make a batch of large tea cakes and keep them in a clean, cloth flour sack. It was always a thrill to reach into that bag and pull out one of her special cookies. Tea cakes have been one of my favorite snacks for many years. In 1983 my husband and I drove to New York City and I took some of these cookies to enjoy on the way. I was excited because I would finally get to study with the great James Beard. During the week we were told that a surprise birthday party was being planned for Mr. Beard and that everyone was to bring a gag gift or a gift from our part of the country. What could be more symbolic of the South than the tea cakes? I purchased a small white box and glued a large red heart on the top. Around the heart I wrote "From the Heart of Dixie." Now every time I enjoy a tea cake, I remember the smile on Mr. Beard's face as he opened his Southern gift.

4 cups self-rising flour
1½ cups sugar
1 cup shortening
½ cup milk
2 eggs
1 teaspoon vanilla extract

Preheat the oven to 425 degrees F.

In a large mixing bowl, combine all the ingredients and beat until well mixed. This will be a sticky, thick mixture. It is easier to roll the dough if it is divided into two or three portions. Spoon out each portion of dough and place it on a well-floured surface. Sprinkle a little flour on top of the dough and carefully form it into a disk. Don't work too much flour into the dough because you want a crisp (short-type) cookie. Roll the dough to a thickness of about ¼ inch. Cut with a 3-inch cookie cutter. Place the cookies on as many ungreased cookie sheets as are available or line the cookie sheets with parchment paper. Space the cookies about 2 inches apart. Don't worry if the cookies are not exactly round because tea cakes don't have to be uniform in shape. Repeat with the remaining dough.

Bake for 7 to 10 minutes, until lightly browned on top. These cookies will be slightly darker around the edge. Remove to a rack to cool. Store in an airtight container.

PEANUT BUTTER COOKIES

Yield: about 4½ dozen cookies

*P*eanut butter cookies will always be special to me because the first recipe that I ever contributed to a cookbook was similar to this one. When I was a teenager, our church was compiling a cookbook as a fund-raiser. I was a novice at baking but I could make peanut butter cookies. It was a thrill to see my recipe in print.

4 tablespoons butter or margarine, softened at room temperature
½ cup peanut butter
½ cup sugar
½ cup firmly packed brown sugar
1 egg
1½ cups all-purpose flour
1 teaspoon baking soda

Preheat the oven to 375 degrees F. Line as many cookie sheets as are available with aluminum foil.

In a large bowl, cream together the butter, peanut butter, sugar, and brown sugar. Add the egg and beat until smooth.

Combine the flour and baking soda in a small bowl. Stir to mix. Gradually add the flour mixture to the creamed mixture. Beat until well mixed.

Form the dough into 1-inch balls. Place the balls about 2 inches apart on the cookie sheets. Flatten to about ¼ inch using a fork in a crisscross pattern. If the fork stick to the dough, dip it into sugar or warm water before pressing the cookies. Bake for 10 to 12 minutes, until lightly browned. Remove immediately from the cookie sheets. Cool on a rack.

Bar Cookies

⋯•◦•◦•◦•◦❄❄C◦•◦•◦•◦•⋯

BROWNIES

Yield: 15 or 16 brownies

*T*here is nothing fancy about these brownies. This is just a basic recipe for fudgelike brownies that are rich and delicious.

¾ cup all-purpose flour
½ teaspoon baking powder
¼ teaspoon salt
2 tablespoons cocoa
1 cup sugar
¼ pound (1 stick) butter or margarine, softened at room temperature
1 teaspoon vanilla extract
2 eggs
⅔ cup chopped walnuts

Preheat the oven to 350 degrees F. Line an 7x11x1-inch baking pan with aluminum foil (or use a 9-inch square pan). Generously grease the foil.

In a large bowl, combine the flour, baking powder, salt, cocoa, sugar, butter, vanilla extract, and eggs. Mix with a spoon just until blended. Stir in the walnuts. Spread in the prepared pan. Bake for 20 minutes, until a wooden pick inserted into center comes out barely moist. Don't overbake. Cool completely before cutting into bars.

NOTE: When lining the pan, use a portion of foil large enough to overhang just a little, so that when the brownies come from the oven you can lift them out of the pan with the foil and cool on a rack without the pan.

CHOCOLATE
PEANUT BUTTER BROWNIES

Yield: 24 brownies (about 2x2¼ inches each)

The aroma of peanut butter as these brownies bake makes it hard to wait until they have cooled before trying one. The texture is cakelike and the taste is definitely chocolate fudge with peanut butter.

¼ pound (1 stick) butter or margarine, softened at room temperature
½ cup peanut butter
1½ cups sugar
1½ teaspoons vanilla extract
3 eggs
1 cup all-purpose flour
¼ cup cocoa

Heat the oven to 350 degrees F. Grease the bottom of a 9x13x2-inch baking pan.

Combine all the ingredients in a large mixing bowl. Beat until blended. The mixture will be a little thick so it will need to be spooned into the pan rather than poured. Spread evenly in pan. Bake for 25 minutes, until a wooden pick inserted into center comes out barely moist. Do not overbake. Cool completely before slicing.

BUTTERSCOTCH BROWNIES

Yield: about 15 brownies

*B*rown sugar gives these chewy brownies that popular butterscotch flavor.

1¼ cups all-purpose flour
1 teaspoon baking powder
¼ teaspoon salt
1 cup firmly packed dark brown sugar
4 tablespoons butter or margarine, softened at room temperature
1 egg
1 teaspoon vanilla extract
½ cup chopped walnuts

Preheat the oven to 350 degrees F. Line a 7x11x1-inch baking pan with aluminum foil. Grease the foil.

Combine the flour, baking powder, and salt in a small bowl. In a large mixing bowl, cream together the brown sugar and butter. Add the egg and vanilla extract. Beat just until blended. Gradually add the flour mixture. Beat until mixed. Stir in the walnuts. This will be a thick batter. Spoon into prepared pan. Spread evenly in pan. Bake for 20 to 25 minutes, or until a wooden pick inserted in the center comes out clean. Do not overbake. Remove from the pan immediately. Remove foil. Cool completely on a rack before cutting into bars.

RAISIN BARS

Yield: 30 bars

Raisins are a great snack right out of the box, but they are also an important ingredient in many recipes. Raisins combined with apple juice and cinnamon make this bar cookie a good lunch box treat.

2 cups raisins
1 cup unsweetened apple juice
¼ pound (1 stick) butter or margarine, softened at room temperature
1½ cups firmly packed brown sugar
2 eggs
2 cups all-purpose flour
1 teaspoon baking soda
¼ teaspoon salt
1½ teaspoons ground cinnamon
1 cup chopped walnuts

APPLE GLAZE

1 cup confectioners' sugar
1½ to 2 tablespoons unsweetened apple juice

Combine the raisins and apple juice in a small saucepan. Bring to a boil. Reduce heat to medium-high and cook until most of the liquid is absorbed. This should take 5 or 6 minutes. Set aside to cool. Drain raisins, reserving 2 tablespoons of the liquid. Pour this liquid back over the raisins.

Preheat the oven to 350 degrees F. Grease and lightly flour a 10x15x1-inch jelly roll pan.

In a large bowl, combine the butter and brown sugar. Beat until well blended. Add the eggs. Beat well.

In a medium bowl, combine the flour, baking soda, salt, and cinnamon. Stir to mix. Gradually add the flour mixture to the creamed mixture, beating well. Stir in the raisins and walnuts. Spread evenly in prepared pan. Bake for about 20 minutes, or until a wooden pick comes out clean when inserted in center. Cool completely.

In a small bowl, combine the glaze ingredients. Beat until smooth. Drizzle over cool raisin bars.

MANDARIN PINEAPPLE BARS

Yield: about 24 bars

A taste of the tropics is captured in these triple-layer bars. A nutty crust is topped with a pineapple-orange filling. A sprinkling of a streusel-like mixture adds a crunchy topping.

CRUST

2 cups all-purpose flour
½ cup sugar
½ cup firmly packed dark brown sugar
¼ teaspoon salt
½ pound (2 sticks) butter or margarine, softened at room temperature
½ cup chopped pecans

TOPPING

¼ cup sugar
¼ cup firmly packed dark brown sugar
2 tablespoons cornstarch
2 egg yolks
⅔ cup well-drained crushed pineapple
⅓ cup pineapple juice
1 cup chopped, canned mandarin oranges

Preheat the oven to 350 degrees F.

Combine the crust ingredients in a large bowl. Mix until crumbly. Reserve ¾ cup of the crumbs. Press the remaining crumbs into the bottom of a 9x13x 2-inch baking pan. Bake for 15 minutes. Allow to cool slightly before adding the topping.

In a medium saucepan, combine the sugar, brown sugar, and cornstarch. Stir to mix well. Add the egg yolks, pineapple, pineapple juice, and mandarin oranges. Stir to mix well. Bring to a boil. Reduce heat to medium and continue cooking, stirring constantly until the mixture thickens. This should take only 1 to 2 minutes. Pour the pineapple mixture over the crust. Sprinkle with the reserved crumbs. Bake for about 30 minutes, until the top crumbs are lightly browned. Cool on a rack before cutting into bars.

ORANGE SLICE AND DATE BARS

....

Yield: 16 (2-inch) bars

*T*hese cookies bring back memories of my childhood. My mother was a member of a ladies' missionary society at our church and I usually went with her to the meetings. Each month one of the members was the hostess and was responsible for the refreshments. I always looked forward to Mrs. Lola May Sanford's turn because these cookies were her specialty. A few years ago I tried to locate the recipe but was unsuccessful, so I decided to see if I could duplicate it from memory. One taste and I knew I had captured that memorable flavor. The orange slices used in this recipe are the jellylike candy slices that are coated with sugar. The best way to cut these orange slices is with kitchen scissors that have been dipped in warm water.

2 tablespoons butter or margarine, softened at room temperature
½ cup firmly packed light brown sugar
1 egg
½ cup plus 2 tablespoons self-rising flour
1 teaspoon vanilla extract
1 cup chopped dates
1 cup chopped candy orange slices
Confectioners' sugar for coating

Preheat the oven to 350 degrees F. Line an 8-inch-square baking pan with aluminum foil. Grease the foil.

In a large bowl, cream together the butter and brown sugar. Add the egg. Beat well. Add the ½ cup of flour and vanilla extract. Mix well. In a medium bowl, combine the dates, orange slices, and the 2 tablespoons of flour. Mix by tossing with your hands to separate the dates and orange slices and to coat them with the flour. Stir the dates and orange slices into the batter. Spread in the prepared pan. Bake for 25 to 30 minutes, until lightly browned.

Turn out of the pan onto a kitchen towel that has been sprinkled generously with confectioners' sugar. Remove the foil. Invert. Sprinkle the top with more confectioners' sugar. Allow to cool before slicing into bars.

Busy Baker Cookies

DROP COOKIES

SHAPED OR ROLLED COOKIES

BAR COOKIES

Drop Cookies

--- ❦ ---

LEMON DROPS

Yield: about 3 dozen small cookies

I developed these cookies when I was on a low-cholesterol diet. This doesn't necessarily mean that they are also low in calories because they do contain oil and sugar.

> 2 cups self-rising flour
> 4 egg whites
> ²/₃ cup canola or safflower oil
> ⅓ cup sugar
> ⅓ cup firmly packed light brown sugar
> 2 teaspoons pure lemon extract

Preheat the oven to 400 degrees F. Line as many cookie sheets as are available with aluminum foil.

Combine all the ingredients in a large bowl. Beat until well mixed. This dough is not as thick as most drop cookie doughs. Drop from a teaspoon onto foil-lined cookie sheets, spacing the cookies about 2 inches apart. Bake for about 8 minutes, or until the cookies begin to brown around the edges. Remove from cookie sheets and cool on a rack.

BUTTERSCOTCH DREAM DROPS

Yield: About 4 dozen cookies

*T*he combination of brown sugar and butterscotch morsels makes these cookies a caramel-lover's dream. They are easy to make using a box of pie crust mix. Pecans and coconut add crunch and flavor.

1 (11 oz.) box pie crust mix
½ teaspoon baking soda
½ cup sugar
½ cup firmly packed light brown sugar
2 eggs
½ cup chopped pecans
½ cup coconut (canned or in plastic bags)
1 cup butterscotch morsels

Heat the oven to 375 degrees F. Line as many cookie sheets as are available with aluminum foil.

In a large bowl, combine the pie crust mix, baking soda, sugars, and eggs. Beat until well mixed. Stir in the pecans, coconut, and butterscotch morsels. Drop from a teaspoon onto foil-lined cookie sheets, spacing the cookies about 2 inches apart. Bake for 8 to 10 minutes, until lightly browned. Immediately remove the cookies from the cookie sheet and cool on a rack.

BUTTERSCOTCH
OATMEAL CRISPIES

Yield: about 4 dozen cookies

A burst of caramel flavor comes through with each bite of these easy-to-make cookies. You will need a food processor for these.

1 (11 oz.) box pie crust mix
1 cup quick-cooking oats (not instant)
1 cup butterscotch morsels
1 cup firmly packed brown sugar
2 eggs
1 cup raisins

Preheat oven to 375 degrees F. Line as many cookie sheets as are available with aluminum foil.

Combine the pie crust mix, oats, butterscotch morsels, and brown sugar in the bowl of a food processor fitted with the steel blade. Process until the texture is very fine. Add the eggs and process until well mixed. Spoon the mixture into a large bowl. Stir in raisins. Drop by rounded teaspoonfuls onto cookie sheets, spacing the cookies about 2 inches apart. Bake for 10 to 12 minutes, until lightly browned. Remove from cookie sheets immediately. Cool on a rack.

CHEWY OATMEAL COOKIES

Yield: about 3½ dozen cookies

*T*hese lightly spiced oatmeal cookies are quick and easy to make using pie crust mix.

1 (11 oz.) box pie crust mix
1⅓ cups firmly packed brown sugar
1½ teaspoons baking powder

½ teaspoon ground cinnamon
2 eggs
1 cup quick-cooking oats (not instant)
½ cup raisins

Preheat the oven to 375 degrees F. Line as many cookie sheets as are available with aluminum foil.

In a large bowl, combine the pie crust mix, brown sugar, baking powder, cinnamon, and eggs. Beat until well mixed. Stir in the oats and raisins. Drop by heaping teaspoonfuls onto foil-lined cookie sheets. Bake for 8 to 10 minutes, until lightly browned. Remove to a rack to cool.

QUICK CHOCOLATE CHIP DELIGHTS

....

Yield: about 4 dozen cookies

*T*hese popular favorites are quick and easy to make but they definitely have that homemade flavor.

1 (11 oz.) box pie crust mix
½ teaspoon baking powder
2 eggs
1 cup firmly packed brown sugar
¾ cup chopped walnuts
1 (6 oz.) package semisweet chocolate morsels

Preheat oven to 375 degrees F. Line as many cookie sheets as are available with aluminum foil.

In a large bowl, combine the pie crust mix, baking powder, eggs, and brown sugar. Beat until well mixed. Stir in the walnuts and chocolate morsels. Drop from a teaspoon onto foil-lined cookie sheets, spacing the cookies about 2 inches apart. Bake for 8 to 10 minutes. Remove the cookies from the foil immediately and cool on a rack.

EASY FRUITCAKE COOKIES

Yield: about 3½ dozen cookies

A box of pie crust mix makes these cookies quick and easy. They taste so homemade that I believe you could fool the pros with them. I don't like a lot of spice in my sweets and have added only a small amount in these cookies. You can increase the spices to suit your own taste. A quick look at the list of ingredients might make you think that this is a hard recipe, when actually it is very easy.

½ cup chopped dates (not the sugared kind)
½ cup chopped candied cherries
½ cup chopped candied pineapple
½ cup raisins
½ cup chopped pecans
1 (11 oz.) box pie crust mix
½ teaspoon baking soda
1 cup sugar
¼ teaspoon ground cinnamon
⅛ teaspoon grated nutmeg
⅛ teaspoon ground cloves
2 eggs

Preheat the oven to 375 degrees F. Line as many cookie sheets as are available with aluminum foil.

In a medium bowl, combine the dates, cherries, pineapple, raisins, and pecans. Mix well.

In a large mixing bowl, combine the pie crust mix, baking soda, sugar, and spices. Stir to mix. Add the eggs and beat well. Stir in the fruit mixture. Mix well. Drop from a teaspoon onto foil-lined cookie sheets, spacing the cookies about 2 inches apart. Bake for about 10 minutes, until light brown. Remove from the cookie sheets and place on a rack to cool completely before storing. Be careful as you remove the cookies from the cookie sheets because they are fragile while hot. They become more crispy as they cool.

DROP TEA CAKES

Yield: about 3½ dozen cookies

*T*his is a quick-and-easy way to make the South's signature cookie, named, I imagine, for the beverage with which they were served. Today, they are enjoyed with coffee, milk, and, still, tea.

2 eggs
⅔ cup vegetable oil
⅔ cup sugar
1 teaspoon vanilla extract
2 cups sifted self-rising flour

Preheat the oven to 400 degrees F. Line as many cookie sheets as are available with aluminum foil.

In a large bowl, beat the eggs until well mixed. Add oil, sugar, vanilla, and flour. Mix well with a spoon. This is a thin mixture. Drop from a teaspoon onto the foil-lined cookie sheets. Bake for 6 to 8 minutes, until lightly browned around the edges. Remove from the cookie sheets and cool on a rack.

Shaped or Rolled Cookies

·····•••••◦◦◦)◦◉◦C(◦◦◦•••••·····

SOUTHERN
PRALINE CRESCENTS

Yield: 24 cookie crescents

These quick-and-easy cookies capture the praline flavor that is so often associated with the South. I prefer the commercially prepared pie crust pastry that is refrigerated, rather than the frozen pie crusts that are packaged in a foil pan. The refrigerated pastry is more like homemade. If you use the frozen pie crusts, allow them to thaw completely and then press the sides down until you get a flat circle of dough.

1 box (2 round pastry sheets) refrigerated pie crust pastry
4 ounces cream cheese, softened
¼ cup firmly packed light brown sugar
⅔ cup finely chopped pecans
1 cup confectioners' sugar

Preheat the oven to 375 degrees F. Allow crusts to come to room temperature. Unfold them.

In a small bowl, combine the cream cheese and brown sugar. Beat until smooth. Spread half the mixture onto each pastry sheet. Sprinkle each with ⅓ cup of the pecans. Using the fingertips, gently press the pecans into the pastry. Cut each pastry into 12 wedges. Starting with the larger end of each pastry wedge, roll toward the small point. Place cookies on two ungreased cookie sheets. Bake for 18 to 20 minutes, until lightly browned. Immediately remove the cookies from the baking sheets and place on a rack. Sprinkle generously with the confectioners' sugar.

MAGIC BERRY BUNDLES

Yield: 18 to 20 cookies

*T*hese are mysterious cookies. Perhaps it is because of humidity or maybe the eggs vary in size (though I use only those sold as large), but I have had two different-looking cookies from this recipe. Both taste the same, they just look different. The first ones I made spread from 1½ inches to 3 inches with a thin layer of preserves in the middle. The next time I made them, they failed to spread and the final result was a small, yet crisp and slightly puffed, cookie with a tiny pocket of preserves in the center. They look like little bundles. The next time, they were thin and large again. Strange, but so fabulous that it doesn't really matter what shape they are.

1 (11 oz.) box pie crust mix

1 cup sugar

1 egg

9 to 10 teaspoons blueberry, strawberry, or blackberry preserves (I usually make some of each)

1 cup confectioners' sugar

Preheat the oven to 375 degrees F. Line as many cookie sheets as are available with aluminum foil.

In a large bowl, combine the pie crust mix, sugar, and egg. Beat until the mixture clings together and can be formed into a ball. On a lightly floured surface, roll the dough to a thickness of about ¼ inch. Cut into small circles using a 1½-inch round cutter. Spoon the preserves into the center of half the cookies, using about ½ teaspoon per cookie. Press the remaining cookies a little with the fingertips to make them large enough to go over the preserves and seal to the bottom cookies. Press around the edges with a fork to seal completely. Place on cookie sheets, spacing them about 3 inches apart. Bake for about 10 to 12 minutes, until lightly browned. Remove from the cookie sheets onto a rack to cool slightly. Coat with confectioners' sugar.

PEANUT BUTTER SNAPS

Yield: about 6 dozen small cookies

*O*nly four ingredients go into these easy peanut butter cookies. My grandson, Steven, likes to make these, and even his little cousin, Paden, can lend a hand. You can have them ready to enjoy in about 20 minutes. In other words, as quick as a snap!

1 (11 oz.) box pie crust mix
1 cup firmly packed light brown sugar
½ cup peanut butter
2 egg whites

Preheat the oven to 375 degrees F. Line as many cookie sheets as are available with aluminum foil.

Combine all the ingredients in the bowl of a food processor fitted with the steel blade. (You can use an electric mixer if you don't have a food processor.) Process until the mixture clings together.

Shape the dough into small balls about 1 inch in diameter. Place on cookie sheets about 2 inches apart. Press each cookie in a crisscross manner using a fork dipped in sugar. Bake for 8 to 10 minutes. Remove from the cookie sheets immediately and cool on a rack.

JIFFY SPRITZ

Yield: about 6 dozen small cookies

$\mathcal{N}$o spritz cookie could be quicker and easier to make. These beautiful butter-type cookies are dainty and crisp. As with any spritz cookies, you will need a cookie press. There are many ways to decorate these cookies. You can sprinkle them with sugar before baking or with a cinnamon-sugar mixture. For the holidays, candied cherries and nuts can be used as decorations. They are also good sandwiched together with peanut butter or chocolate frosting.

1 (11 oz.) box pie crust mix
1 cup sugar
1 egg
1 teaspoon vanilla extract (or any other flavoring you might like)
1 tablespoon water (only if needed)

Preheat the oven to 375 degrees F. Line as many cookie sheets as are available with aluminum foil.

Combine the pie crust mix, sugar, egg, and flavoring. Beat until well blended. If the mixture is not soft enough to use in the cookie press, add the tablespoon of water and mix. Fill the cookie press with the soft dough. Press cookies onto the cookie sheets, spacing them about 2 inches apart. Bake for 8 to 10 minutes, or until the cookies begin to brown around the edges. Remove from the cookie sheets immediately and cool on a rack.

Bar Cookies

⋯⋯⋯⋯⋯⋯⋯⋯⋯⋯⋯

EASY BRICKLE BROWNIES

Yield: about 15 brownies

*I*n most brownie recipes, we are instructed to "mix only until the dry ingredients are moistened." This quick-and-easy version is an exception. A mixer is used and the batter is beaten until it looks almost like chocolate mousse. Almond brickle chips add a crispy texture to these fudgy brownies.

1 cup sugar
3 tablespoons cocoa
½ cup all-purpose flour
¼ pound (1 stick) butter or margarine, softened at room temperature
2 eggs
1 teaspoon vanilla extract
½ cup almond brickle chips
½ cup sliced almonds, coarsely broken

Preheat the oven to 325 degrees F. Grease a 7x11x1-inch baking pan.

Combine the sugar, cocoa, flour, butter, eggs, and vanilla extract in a large bowl. Beat for 3 minutes at medium speed. Stir in the brickle chips and almonds. Spoon into the prepared pan and smooth the top. Bake for 25 to 28 minutes. Avoid overbaking, testing with a wooden pick inserted near the center; when it comes out barely moist, the brownies are done. Cool completely in the pan before cutting into bars.

STRAWBERRY CHEESECAKE BARS

Yield: about 50 small bars

I like anything that tastes like cheesecake, and a strawberry flavor makes it even more enticing. These bars are so rich that a small portion will satisfy the sweet tooth.

1 (18.25 oz.) box strawberry cake mix
½ cup chopped pecans
¼ pound (1 stick) butter or margarine, softened at room temperature
2 eggs
1 (16 oz.) box confectioners' sugar
8 ounces cream cheese, softened at room temperature
1 tablespoon strawberry preserves

Preheat the oven to 350 degrees F. Grease a 9x13x2-inch baking pan.

In a large bowl, combine the cake mix, pecans, butter, and 1 of the eggs. Mix well and press into pan.

In a medium bowl, combine the remaining egg with the confectioners' sugar, cream cheese, and strawberry preserves. Beat until smooth. Pour over the strawberry "crust." Bake for 45 minutes, until cheesecake topping is set and is lightly browned. Allow to cool completely before slicing. Cut into 1x2-inch bars.

CARAMEL CHERRY
GRAHAM CRISPS

....

Yield: about 150 1-inch squares

*T*hese cookies are a snap to make. After the pecans and cherries are chopped, it takes only about 10 minutes from start to finish to have a batch of these wonderful treats ready.

12 (2½x5-inch) graham crackers
2 cups miniature marshmallows
¾ cup firmly packed dark brown sugar
12 tablespoons (1½ sticks) butter or margarine
1 teaspoon ground cinnamon
1 teaspoon vanilla extract
¾ cup chopped pecans
¾ cup chopped candied cherries
¾ cup coconut (canned or in plastic bags)

Preheat the oven to 350 degrees F. Place the graham crackers in a 10x15x1-inch jelly roll pan. Sprinkle the marshmallows over the crackers.

Combine the brown sugar, butter, and cinnamon in a small saucepan. Heat until the sugar is dissolved and the butter has melted. Remove from the heat. Stir in the vanilla extract. Pour this mixture over the crackers and marshmallows. Combine the pecans, cherries, and coconut. Sprinkle on top of caramel mixture. Bake for about 5 minutes, or until the topping is bubbly and the marshmallows begin to melt. Remove from the oven and place on a rack to cool. Cut into small squares.

CHEESY GERMAN CHOCOLATE BARS

Yield: 18 bars (about 1½x4 inches each)

These fudgy bar cookies made from a cake mix taste like the famous German chocolate cake, with cream cheese added as an accent flavor.

1 box German chocolate cake mix
2 eggs
¼ pound (1 stick) butter or margarine, softened at room temperature
8 ounces cream cheese, softened at room temperature
1 cup firmly packed light brown sugar
⅔ cup flaked coconut (canned or in plastic bags)
¾ cup chopped pecans

Preheat the oven to 350 degrees F. Grease a 9x13x2-inch baking pan.

In a large bowl, combine the cake mix, 1 of the eggs, and butter. Mix until crumbly. Press into the prepared pan.

In another bowl, combine the cream cheese, brown sugar, and remaining egg. Beat until smooth. Stir in the coconut and pecans. Spread this mixture over the "crust." Bake for 35 to 40 minutes, until cheesy topping is set and lightly browned. Allow to cool in the pan before slicing.

Pies, Puddings,
AND
Other Desserts

If you want to make a Southern dessert lover happy, bring out a slice of rich pie or a bowl of fruit cobbler topped with whipped cream or ice cream. As one New York pastry chef remarked, "It seems that Southerners have an ongoing love affair with desserts." This is true.

Some of the pies of my youth that are as popular today as they were then are pecan, coconut cream, chocolate cream, banana cream, apple, and blueberry. I've included cobblers here because Southerners consider them pies. In addition to the traditional berry and fruit cobblers, one all-time favorite from the past is the slightly spicy sweet potato cobbler.

A lot of novice bakers shy away from pies because they fear pastry. I fell into this category myself for many years. When I decided to try and try again until I succeeded at pastry making, however, I was surprised that I so quickly mastered it. There is a feeling of accomplishment when you tackle a dreaded task and succeed. This is the way I felt after learning to make pie crusts.

If you definitely don't want to bake pie crusts, you might like to try the simple meringue-type pies in the Busy Baker section. There are several of these. Each is easy, quick, and elegant. These include choco-mint pie, Lady Baltimore pie, and mystery chocolate chip pie. In this same section, you will find an easy "stir-and-pour" cobbler and another made with a crust of refrigerated cinnamon roll dough. In this cookbook, there are pies for all bakers.

Another baked dessert that delights the Southern palate is the custard. In the South, two custard favorites, egg and sweet potato, are usually baked in a crust, so perhaps these are really pies rather than baked custards. Regardless of the category, Southerners love them.

Custards baked in a water bath are not as popular in the South as boiled custards or the custard pies, but they are occasionally found on Southern tables for special events.

When I was growing up, my mother practiced frugality out of necessity. Using the basic food staples that we had on hand, she could turn simple ingredients into delicious desserts.

One of my favorite frugal desserts is bread pudding. Breads can vary from leftover baked biscuits to French bread that has become a little stale. Add milk, sugar, eggs, and vanilla extract and you have a delicious inexpensive dessert. If you have some raisins, add a few to the bread pudding. Most bread puddings are served with a sauce, but some Southerners still prefer to serve them simply with milk.

Rice pudding is made in much the same way as bread pudding, substituting cooked white rice for the bread. Fruits can be added for extra flavor.

Windowsill Favorites

PIES

OTHER BAKED DESSERTS

Pies

COCONUT CREAM PIE

Yield: 8 servings

*W*ith the exception of chocolate and banana cream, there's no other cream pie that can tempt the palate quite like coconut cream. The chewy texture of the coconut combined with the extra smooth custard make this a taste bud thrill.

BASIC PIE CRUST

¼ cup chilled shortening
4 tablespoons chilled butter or margarine
1½ cups all-purpose flour
3 to 4 tablespoons ice water

COCONUT CREAM FILLING

⅔ cup sugar
4 tablespoons all-purpose flour
¼ teaspoon salt
3 egg yolks (save whites for the meringue)
1½ cups milk
1 teaspoon vanilla extract
1 tablespoon butter or margarine
1½ cups coconut (canned or in plastic bags)

BASIC MERINGUE

3 egg whites
¼ teaspoon cream of tartar
6 tablespoons sugar

Cut the shortening and butter into the flour using a food processor, pastry blender, or two knives. The mixture should resemble coarse cornmeal with a few lumps about the size of peas. Gradually add the ice water, mixing until the dough can be formed into a smooth ball. Shape into a disk, cover with plastic wrap, and refrigerate for about 30 minutes.

Preheat the oven to 425 degrees F.

Roll out the chilled dough on a lightly floured surface to a circle larger than a 9-inch pie plate. Place the pastry in the pie plate. Trim the edges, leaving an overhang of about ¾ inch. Turn this edge under, making a thick rim for fluting. If you don't like to flute the edges, simply press the edge with a fork.

Fit a piece of aluminum foil over the crust. Fill with pie weights or dried beans. Bake for about 5 minutes. Remove the foil and weights. Continue baking for an additional 5 minutes, or until the crust is lightly browned. Remove from the oven and place on a rack.

To make the filling, combine the sugar, flour, and salt in a heavy saucepan. Mix well, using the back of the spoon to break up any small lumps of flour. Add the egg yolks but don't mix yet. As you gradually add the milk, stir the yolks into the dry ingredients until you get a smooth mixture. Cook over medium to medium-high heat, stirring constantly, for about 5 minutes, or until thickened. Remove from the heat. Stir in the vanilla, butter, and coconut. Pour into the baked pie shell.

Preheat the oven to 350 degrees F.

Beat the egg whites until foamy. Add the cream of tartar and continue beating until the egg whites form a soft peak. Gradually add the sugar, beating well after each addition. Continue beating until stiff peaks form and the sugar is completely dissolved. To test this, rub a small amount of the meringue between the finger and thumb. If it feels grainy, continue beating. Smooth over the pie and bake until the meringue is lightly browned, about 10 minutes.

CHOCOLATE CREAM PIE
IN PEANUT BUTTER CRUST

Yield: 8 servings

Chocolate and peanut butter are a perfect flavor duo. The small amount of peanut butter in the crust adds just a hint of peanut flavor to this popular pie.

PEANUT BUTTER CRUST

⅓ cup chilled shortening
2 tablespoons chilled peanut butter
1½ cups all-purpose flour
3 or 4 tablespoons ice water

CHOCOLATE PIE FILLING

1 cup sugar
3 tablespoons cocoa
¼ cup all-purpose flour
⅛ teaspoon salt
3 egg yolks
1½ cups milk
1 teaspoon vanilla extract
2 tablespoons butter or margarine

MERINGUE

3 egg whites
¼ teaspoon cream of tartar
6 tablespoons sugar

To make the crust, cut the shortening and peanut butter into the flour using a food processor, pastry blender, or two knives. Gradually add the ice water, mixing until the dough forms a ball. Form into a disk, cover with plastic wrap, and refrigerate for about 30 minutes.

To make the filling, combine the sugar, cocoa, flour, and salt in a heavy saucepan. Mix well, using the back of a spoon to break up any small lumps of flour or cocoa. Add the yolks and gradually stir in the milk until the mixture is smooth. Place over medium to medium-high heat and cook, stirring constantly, for about 5 minutes, or until the mixture thickens. Remove from the heat. Stir in vanilla and butter.

Preheat the oven to 350 degrees F. Remove the dough from the refrigerator and roll out on a lightly floured surface until pastry circle is at least an inch larger than the 9-inch pie plate. Bake with aluminum foil and pie weights according to directions in coconut cream pie recipe on page 141. Pour the filling into baked pie crust.

To make the meringue, beat the egg whites until foamy. Add the cream of tartar and continue beating until the egg whites form soft peaks. Gradually add the sugar, beating well after each addition. Continue beating until stiff peaks form and the sugar is completely dissolved. To test this, rub a small amount of the meringue between the finger and thumb. If it feels grainy, continue beating. Smooth over the pie filling and bake until the meringue is lightly browned, about 10 minutes.

BANANA PRALINE CREAM PIE

Yield 8 servings

*T*wo things make this version of banana cream pie unusual. The custard is made with brown sugar, giving it a butterscotch or caramel flavor, and almond brickle chips are stirred in to give it a little crunch. Almond brickle chips can also be sprinkled on the pie crust underneath the bananas, if desired.

½ cup sugar
½ cup firmly packed light brown sugar
5 tablespoons all-purpose flour
3 egg yolks
1½ cups milk
1 teaspoon vanilla extract
1 cup almond brickle chips
2 medium bananas
1 (9-inch) pie crust, baked (pages 140–141)

MERINGUE

3 egg whites
¼ teaspoon cream of tartar
6 tablespoons sugar

Combine the sugar, brown sugar, and flour in a heavy saucepan. Stir to mix using the back of the spoon to mash any lumps of flour. Add the egg yolks and gradually work them into the sugar mixture as you add the milk. Mix well. Cook over medium heat for about 5 minutes, or until the mixture thickens. The custard will need to be stirred constantly to prevent scorching. Remove from heat. Stir in the vanilla. Allow the mixture to cool. Stir in the almond brickle chips. Slice the bananas and place in the bottom of the baked pie crust. Pour the custard on top of the bananas.

Preheat the oven to 350 degrees F.

To make the meringue, beat the egg whites until foamy. Add the cream of tartar and continue beating until stiff peaks form and the sugar is completely dissolved. To test this, rub a small amount of the meringue between the finger and thumb. If it feels grainy, continue beating. Smooth over the pie filling and bake until the meringue is lightly browned, about 10 minutes. If desired, sprinkle meringue with sliced or chopped almonds before baking.

NOTE: To prevent the bananas from turning dark, sprinkle with a little lemon juice, if desired.

PEANUT FUDGE PIE

Yield: 8 to 10 servings

This pie will thrill the palate of the chocoholic. It is rich, creamy, and chocolate! A small scoop of vanilla ice cream on the side would add the final touch to this super chocolate pie. If you like a lighter chocolate, try it with sweet chocolate instead of semisweet. The unsalted roasted peanuts add a delightful crunch plus a flavor bonus.

4 tablespoons butter or margarine, softened at room temperature
1 cup sugar
¼ cup all-purpose flour
1 teaspoon vanilla extract
3 eggs
8 ounces semisweet chocolate, melted
1 cup chopped, unsalted roasted peanuts
1 (9-inch) basic pie crust, unbaked (pages 140–141)

Preheat the oven to 375 degrees F.

In a large mixing bowl, combine the butter, sugar, flour, and vanilla. Beat until mixture resembles pie crust dough. Add the eggs one at a time, beating well after each addition. Add melted chocolate. Mix well. Stir in the peanuts. Pour into unbaked pie crust. Bake for about 30 minutes, or until the filling is set and the top is firm and crispy. Cool completely on a rack before slicing.

LEMON MACAROON PIE

Yield: about 8 servings

*A*s the pie bakes, the coconut rises to the top of this delicately flavored lemon custard. Unsweetened macaroon coconut is best for this pie because it has a very fine texture. It is usually available at health food stores, but if you can't find it, you can substitute a homemade version, which is made by processing flaked or shredded coconut (not fresh or frozen) in a food processor until it is fine. The flaked or shredded coconut that you buy at the local supermarket is usually sweetened, but the amount of sugar is so small that it really doesn't make a noticeable change in the pie filling.

CRUST

1¼ cups all-purpose flour
¼ teaspoon salt
1 teaspoon sugar
⅓ cup chilled shortening
2 to 4 tablespoons ice water

LEMON MACAROON FILLING

3 eggs
1½ cups sugar
6 tablespoons unsalted butter, melted
¼ teaspoon salt
1 teaspoon vanilla extract
3 tablespoons freshly squeezed lemon juice
1 cup fine macaroon coconut

Combine the flour, salt, and sugar in the bowl of a food processor fitted with the steel blade. Pulse two or three times to aerate. Add the shortening. Pulse until the mixture resembles coarse meal. Stop the processor. Add the water, starting with 2 tablespoons, and then add the remainder as needed. Process until the mixture forms a ball. Shape the dough into a disk 4 to 5 inches in diameter. Cover with plastic wrap. Refrigerate for at least 30 minutes.

On a lightly floured surface, roll the dough to a circle about 10 inches in diameter and ⅛ inch thick. Fit the dough into a 9-inch pie plate. Trim the crust about 1 inch larger than the pie plate. Turn the edge under and flute, if desired. Place in the freezer while preparing the filling.

Preheat the oven to 400 degrees F.

For the filling, combine the eggs, sugar, melted butter, salt, vanilla extract, and lemon juice. Beat until well mixed. Stir in the coconut.

Remove the pie shell from the freezer. Pour the filling into the pie shell. Bake at 400 degrees F. for 10 minutes. Immediately reduce the temperature to 350 degrees F. and continue baking for an additional 35 to 40 minutes, until the filling is set and the top is browned. Cool completely before slicing.

LEMON CHESS PIE

Yield: 8 servings

*I*t is believed that chess pie is of British origin; it was certainly adapted to the Southern palate as far back as the colonial period. With a few staples in the kitchen pantry, the plantation cook could make this simple pie for any unexpected dinner guests. The small amount of cornmeal used in the pie gives the filling a granular appearance, but the taste is definitely not grainy.

2 cups sugar
1 tablespoon all-purpose flour
1 tablespoon cornmeal
4 eggs
4 tablespoons butter, melted
3 to 4 tablespoons freshly squeezed lemon juice
1 teaspoon grated lemon peel
¼ cup milk
1 (9-inch) basic pie crust, unbaked (pages 140–141)

Preheat the oven to 350 degrees F.

In a large mixing bowl, combine the sugar, flour, and cornmeal. Stir to mix. Add the eggs. Beat well. Add the butter, lemon juice, lemon peel, and milk. Beat well. Pour the filling into the unbaked pie crust. Bake for 50 to 55 minutes, until the filling is set in the center and the top is golden brown. Remove from the oven and cool before slicing.

LEMON MERINGUE PIE

Yield: 8 servings

*T*his is a basic lemon pie, similar to any recipe you might find in old cookbooks.

⅓ cup cornstarch
1½ cups sugar
¼ teaspoon salt
4 egg yolks
2 cups hot water
¼ cup freshly squeezed lemon juice
1 tablespoon butter
1 (9-inch) basic pie crust, baked (pages 140–141)

MERINGUE

3 egg whites
¼ teaspoon cream of tartar
6 tablespoons sugar

Preheat the oven to 350 degrees F.

Combine the cornstarch, sugar, salt, and egg yolks in a medium saucepan. Stir to mix well. Stir in the hot water. Cook over medium heat until thick, stirring constantly to prevent scorching. Remove from heat. Stir in lemon juice and butter. Pour into crust.

To make the meringue, beat the egg whites until foamy. Add the cream of tartar and continue beating until stiff peaks form and the sugar is completely dissolved. To test this, rub a small amount of the meringue between the finger and thumb. If it feels grainy, continue beating.

Spoon the meringue on top of the lemon filling. Bake for 15 to 20 minutes, until delicately browned. Cool completely before slicing. Keep refrigerated.

BUTTERMILK PIE

Yield: 8 servings

*B*uttermilk pie is a very old Southern favorite. Some recipes call for raisins, and others add coconut to this basic recipe. I remember one time when I wanted to bake this pie but didn't have enough buttermilk. I looked in the refrigerator and saw some sour cream and a carton of skim milk. I mixed the two in equal proportions and the pie turned out great.

3 eggs
1 cup sugar
¼ teaspoon salt
1 teaspoon vanilla extract
1 cup buttermilk
1 (9-inch) basic pie crust, unbaked (pages 140–141)

Preheat the oven to 375 degrees F.

Combine the eggs and sugar in a large bowl. Beat until light, or about 1 minute with an electric mixer. Add salt, vanilla, and buttermilk. Mix well. Pour into unbaked pie crust. Bake for 30 to 35 minutes, or until a knife comes out clean when inserted into the center of the pie. Cool completely before cutting.

NOTE: This does not make a deep pie.

PEANUT BUTTER PIE

Yield: 8 to 10 servings

This unusual pie tastes as if it is made with peanut butter, but it is melted peanut butter morsels that give the pie that ever popular flavor. A little whipped cream is just what this pie needs to make it extra special.

CHOCOLATE PEANUT CRUST

1½ cups all-purpose flour
1 tablespoon cocoa
⅓ cup ground, unsalted, roasted peanuts
4 tablespoons chilled butter or margarine
¼ cup chilled shortening
3 to 5 tablespoons ice water

PEANUT BUTTER FILLING

4 tablespoons butter or margarine, softened at room temperature
1 cup sugar
¼ cup all-purpose flour
1 teaspoon vanilla extract
3 eggs
8 ounces peanut butter morsels, melted
1 cup heavy cream, whipped (optional)
½ cup chopped roasted peanuts (optional)

Combine the flour, cocoa, and ground peanuts. Stir to mix. Cut the butter and shortening into the flour mixture, using a food processor fitted with the steel blade, two knives, or a pastry blender. Add the ice water a tablespoon at a time, mixing until the dough forms a ball. Chill for 15 to 20 minutes.

Remove the dough from the refrigerator and allow to soften just enough to roll out on a lightly floured surface to a circle about 2 inches larger than a 9-inch pie pan. Fit the crust into the pan. Trim the edges to about 1-inch overhang. Fold edge of dough under to make a double-thick rim. Flute.

Preheat the oven to 425 degrees F.

For the filling, combine the butter, sugar, flour, and vanilla in a large bowl. Beat until the mixture resembles pie crust. Add the eggs one at a time, beating well after each addition. Add the melted butterscotch morsels. Beat until smooth. Pour into crust. Bake for about 5 minutes at 425 degrees F. Reduce temperature to 350 degrees F. and continue baking for 20 to 25 minutes, or until a thin knife blade comes out clean when inserted into the center of the pie. Remove from oven. Cool completely on a rack before slicing. Serve with whipped cream sprinkled with chopped roasted peanuts, if desired.

OATMEAL PIE

Yield: 8 servings

*T*his is an economical stand-in for pecan pie. As the pie bakes, the oats rise and form a crunchy topping that, at first glance, looks like a pecan pie. Very tasty substitute!

1 cup light corn syrup
1 cup firmly packed light brown sugar
4 tablespoons butter or margarine, melted
1 teaspoon vanilla extract
⅛ teaspoon salt
1½ cups oats (not instant)
1 (9-inch) basic pie crust, unbaked (pages 140–141)

Preheat the oven to 350 degrees F.

Combine the corn syrup, brown sugar, butter, vanilla, and salt in a large bowl. Beat until blended. Stir in the oats.

Pour the mixture into the unbaked pie crust. Bake for 1 hour. If the edges of the crust begin to brown too much, put strips of aluminum foil around them to prevent further browning. Cool completely before slicing.

SOUTHERN PECAN PIE

Yield 8 servings

Southerners like their desserts rich, so it is not surprising that pecan pie is a favorite. The filling in this pie is so dark that you might think that it has some chocolate in it, but it doesn't. If you prefer a lighter colored filling, simply substitute light brown sugar for the dark brown and use only light corn syrup.

1 cup firmly packed dark brown sugar
1 tablespoon all-purpose flour
3 eggs
½ cup dark corn syrup
½ cup light corn syrup
1 teaspoon vanilla extract
4 tablespoons butter or margarine, melted
1 cup chopped pecans
1 (9-inch) basic pie crust, unbaked (pages 140–141)

Preheat the oven to 350 degrees F.

Combine the brown sugar and flour in a small bowl. Mix well. In a large bowl, combine the eggs, corn syrups, vanilla, and melted butter. Beat with a fork. Add the sugar mixture and mix well.

Sprinkle the pecans over the bottom of the pie crust. Pour the filling on top of the pecans. As the pie bakes, the pecans will rise to the top. Bake for 55 to 60 minutes, until filling is set and pecans are golden brown. Cool before slicing.

PINEAPPLE PECAN PIE

Yield: 8 servings

$\mathcal{P}$ineapple ice cream topping turns pecan pie into a tropical delight. The topping replaces the corn syrup in the original pecan pie recipe.

1 cup firmly packed light brown sugar
1 tablespoon all-purpose flour
3 eggs
1 cup pineapple ice cream topping
1 teaspoon vanilla extract
4 tablespoons butter or margarine, melted
1 cup chopped pecans
1 (9-inch) basic pie crust, unbaked (pages 140–141)

Preheat the oven to 350 degrees F.

In a small bowl, combine the brown sugar and flour. Mix well. Combine the eggs, pineapple topping, vanilla, and melted butter. Beat until well mixed. Add the brown sugar mixture and beat well. Stir in the pecans. Pour into the unbaked pie crust. Bake for 1 hour, until filling is set and pecans are golden brown.

ORANGE WALNUT PIE

Yield: 8 servings

This is a super-rich pie that is a delight to the taste buds. The tartness of the orange marmalade adds zing to the pie.

3 eggs
½ cup light corn syrup
½ cup orange marmalade
⅔ cup firmly packed light brown sugar
4 tablespoons butter or margarine, melted
1½ cups chopped walnuts
1 (9-inch) basic pie crust, (pages 140–141)

Preheat the oven to 350 degrees F.

Combine the eggs, corn syrup, orange marmalade, brown sugar, and melted butter in a large bowl. Beat until well mixed. Stir in the walnuts. Pour into the unbaked pie crust. Bake for 50 to 55 minutes, or until filling is set. If the pie crust seems to be browning too quickly, cover edges with a strip of foil to prevent further browning.

PEACHY CREAM CHEESE PIE

Yield: 8 servings

A thin layer of fresh peaches hidden under a smooth cream cheese topping makes this pie taste like an upside-down cheesecake.

1 cup mashed fresh peaches (about the consistency of crushed pineapple)
1 cup sugar
1 tablespoon cornstarch
8 ounces cream cheese, softened at room temperature
2 eggs
½ cup milk
½ teaspoon vanilla extract
1 (9-inch) basic pie crust, unbaked (pages 140–141)
½ cup chopped pecans

Preheat the oven to 425 degrees F.

Combine the peaches, ½ cup of the sugar, and the cornstarch in a medium saucepan. Cook over medium-high heat, stirring constantly, until thickened (this should take 2 to 3 minutes). Cool.

Beat the cream cheese with the remaining ½ cup sugar, blending well. Add the eggs one at a time, mixing well after each addition. Add milk and vanilla. Mix well.

Spread the cooled peach mixture over the bottom of the unbaked pie crust. Pour the cream cheese mixture over the peaches. Sprinkle the pecans on top.

Bake for 10 minutes at 425 degrees F. Reduce the heat to 325 degrees F. and continue baking for an additional 45 to 50 minutes, until cheese layer is set and lightly browned. Cool completely before slicing.

NOTE: The pie will puff up during baking and it will sometimes have small cracks on top. Don't worry. When it cools, the filling sinks a little and the cracks are barely noticeable.

FRESH BLUEBERRY PIE

Yield: 8 servings

*I*t is always a thrill when blueberries are in season because that means it's time for a special pie. This is a very basic and simple recipe that anyone can make. The pecan pastry adds a wonderful flavor accent, but if you don't like to make pie crusts, pick up a couple of frozen pie crusts at the supermarket. Pour the filling into one and press the remaining, thawed crust over the top.

PECAN PASTRY

3 cups all-purpose flour
½ cup ground pecans
½ teaspoon baking powder
½ teaspoon salt
½ cup chilled vegetable shortening
¼ pound (1 stick) chilled butter or margarine
5 to 6 tablespoons ice water

FILLING

4 cups fresh blueberries, washed and drained
1 cup sugar
¼ cup all-purpose flour
2 tablespoons butter or margarine

Combine the flour, pecans, baking powder, and salt in a large bowl or in the bowl of a food processor fitted with the steel blade. Stir to mix. Cut in the shortening and butter until the mixture resembles coarse cornmeal with just a few lumps the size of peas. Gradually add the ice water and mix until the dough can be formed into a smooth ball. If you are using a food processor, the ball will form automatically when enough water has been added. Divide the dough in half, making two disks each about an inch thick. Cover with plastic wrap. Chill for about 30 minutes.

Preheat the oven to 450 degrees F. Remove the dough from the refrigerator and allow to sit until soft enough to roll without tearing. Roll each disk to a circle an inch or two larger than a 9-inch pie plate. Fit one circle of dough in the pie pan.

Combine the blueberries, sugar, and flour in a medium bowl. Toss lightly to coat the berries. Pour into pie crust. Dot with butter. Top with the second circle of dough. Trim and flute the edges of the crust. Cut 5 or 6 small slits in the top crust to allow steam to escape. Bake for 10 minutes at 450 degrees F., then lower the temperature to 350 degrees F. and continue baking for about 30 minutes. If the edges of the crust seem to be browning too quickly, cover them with aluminum foil the last 10 or 15 minutes of baking. Allow to cool completely before slicing.

SCOTCH AND ALE APPLE PIE

....

Yield: 8 servings

*E*ven though it sounds as if there are alcoholic beverages in this pie, there isn't a drop. The "scotch" is the butterscotch in the cookielike crust, and the "ale" is the ginger ale in which the apples are cooked. The filling will be soft so the pie might not cut with a smooth edge.

BUTTERSCOTCH CRUST

½ cup butterscotch morsels
1¼ cups all-purpose flour
⅛ teaspoon salt
¾ cup chopped walnuts
¼ pound (1 stick) butter or margarine, softened at room temperature

FILLING

¾ cup ginger ale
½ cup sugar
2 teaspoons lemon juice
3½ cups peeled and chopped Granny Smith apples
8 ounces cream cheese, softened at room temperature
2 cups confectioners' sugar
½ cup heavy cream, whipped

Preheat the oven to 350 degrees F. Combine the butterscotch morsels, flour, salt, and walnuts in the bowl of a food processor fitted with the steel

(continued)

blade. Process until the mixture is almost as fine as flour. Add the butter and process until mixed. Press the mixture into a 9-inch pie plate. Bake for about 15 minutes, until lightly browned. The crust will shrink slightly and probably puff up a little, but don't worry. As soon as the crust comes from the oven, quickly reshape it with your fingertips and flatten the puffy part. It will become crisper as it cools. Cool completely before adding the filling.

Combine the ginger ale, sugar, lemon juice, and chopped apples in a medium pan. Cook over medium-high heat until tender but not mushy. This should take 3 to 4 minutes. Remove from heat. Drain. Cool completely.

In a large mixing bowl, combine the cream cheese and confectioners' sugar. Beat until smooth. Stir in the whipped cream. Add the cooled apple mixture. Spoon into pie crust. Refrigerate.

OLD-FASHIONED APPLE PIE

Yield: about 8 servings

*T*he phrase "as American as" is almost always followed by "apple pie." It's not surprising that apple pie is one of the most popular desserts in our country and has been for hundreds of years. Top it with a scoop of vanilla ice cream, a dollop of whipped cream, or a thin slice of Cheddar and you have a dessert to be remembered for a long time. I have learned that adding a little baking powder to pie crust pastry tends to make a flaky but more compact crust that is especially good for moist fruit fillings.

DOUBLE CRUST PASTRY
3 cups all-purpose flour
¾ teaspoon baking powder
¼ teaspoon salt
½ cup chilled shortening
¼ pound (1 stick) chilled butter or margarine
5 to 6 tablespoons ice water

FILLING

1 cup sugar
¼ cup all-purpose flour
½ teaspoon ground cinnamon
6 cups peeled and sliced Granny Smith apples (5 or 6 apples)
2 tablespoons butter or margarine
2 tablespoons heavy cream

Combine the flour, baking powder, and salt in the bowl of a food processor fitted with the steel blade. Pulse two or three times to mix. Add the shortening and butter. Pulse until the mixture looks like coarse cornmeal with just a few lumps about the size of peas. Add the ice water gradually and process until the mixture forms a ball. Remove from the bowl and shape into two disks. Cover with plastic wrap. Refrigerate for about 30 minutes.

To make the filling, combine the sugar, flour, and cinnamon. Mix well. Sprinkle over apples and stir to coat.

Preheat the oven to 400 degrees F. Roll out each portion of pastry to a circle about an inch larger than a 9-inch pie pan. Fit one crust in the pan. Trim the edges and fill with the apples. Dot with butter. Wet the rim of the bottom crust with water. Place the remaining crust on top. Trim and seal to the bottom crust by pressing around the edges with a fork. Brush the top with cream to give it a delicately browned crust. Stick a fork into the top crust several times or cut small slits to allow steam to escape during baking. Bake for 50 to 60 minutes. To prevent the crust from browning too fast, cover the top loosely with a piece of aluminum foil for the last 10 minutes of baking time. Allow to cool before slicing.

PUMPKIN PIE

Yield: 6 to 8 servings

*P*umpkin pie is a holiday favorite from coast to coast, and this one will certainly be a hit with your family and friends. Its special flavor comes from piña colada mixer, which adds a hint of the tropics.

2½ cups cooked, mashed pumpkin (or canned pumpkin purée)
¼ pound (1 stick) butter or margarine, softened at room temperature
⅔ cup firmly packed light brown sugar
⅓ cup piña colada mixer
2 eggs
1 teaspoon vanilla extract
¼ teaspoon ground cinnamon
⅛ teaspoon grated nutmeg
1 (9-inch) basic pie crust, unbaked (pages 140–141)

Preheat the oven to 400 degrees F.

In a large mixing bowl, combine the pumpkin, butter, brown sugar, and piña colada mixer. Beat until well mixed. Add the eggs and beat well. Stir in the vanilla extract, cinnamon, and nutmeg. Pour the filling into the unbaked pie crust. Bake at 400 degrees F. for 10 minutes. Reduce temperature to 350 degrees F. and continue baking for an additional 30 to 35 minutes, or until a thin knife blade comes out clean when inserted into the center of the pie. Cool completely before slicing.

TYLER PIE

Yield: 6 to 8 servings

*O*ur tenth president, John Tyler, was said to have enjoyed a pie similar to this one bearing his name. The northern version is often made with maple syrup. In the South, sorghum syrup or unsulfured molasses is the preferred sweetener. I like to tone down the strong flavor of the sorghum by substituting some sugar for a portion of the syrup.

¾ cup sorghum syrup (or unsulfured molasses)
¾ cup sugar
4 tablespoons butter or margarine, melted
½ cup heavy cream
3 eggs, slightly beaten
1½ teaspoons vanilla extract
½ teaspoon pure lemon extract
¼ teaspoon ground cinnamon
1 (9-inch) basic pie crust, unbaked (pages 140–141)

Preheat the oven to 400 degrees F.

In a large mixing bowl, combine the syrup, sugar, butter, and cream. Beat until well blended. Add the eggs, extracts, and cinnamon. Mix well. Pour into the unbaked pie crust. Bake at 400 degrees F. for 10 minutes. Reduce the temperature to 350 degrees F. and continue baking for another 35 to 40 minutes, or until a thin knife blade comes out clean when inserted near the center of the pie.

NOTE: If the rim of the pie crust seems to be browning too quickly, cover the edges with aluminum foil.

SOUTHERN EGG CUSTARD PIE

Yield: 6 to 8 servings

*L*earning to make an egg custard was a memorable event for me. I received a call from a lady who wanted a recipe for an old-fashioned egg custard with a silky smooth texture. Knowing my love for baking, she felt sure that I would have the recipe. I was too embarrassed to admit that I had only made one egg custard in my life and wasn't particularly proud of it. I promised to send her the recipe but there was just one problem. I had to learn to make an egg custard. I read everything I could find about this traditional Southern dessert. You can imagine my delight as I sliced the third custard and saw that silky smooth texture with a cut edge that shined like satin.

Now I don't know why I feared egg custard because it is easy to make if a few simple steps are followed. It is important not to overbeat the custard. A gentle mixing with a fork is all that is needed. A low oven temperature is another factor. And finally, the use of cheesecloth keeps the filling smooth and silky. Egg custard has always been one of my husband's favorite desserts so you can imagine his delight when I finally learned to make a good one.

5 eggs
1 cup sugar
1 tablespoon butter or margarine, melted
1¼ cups milk
¾ teaspoon vanilla extract
1 (9-inch) basic pie crust, unbaked (pages 140–141)
½ teaspoon grated nutmeg

Preheat the oven to 325 degrees F.

In a large mixing bowl, beat the eggs slightly using a fork. It is important not to overbeat. Add the sugar and melted butter. Stir until mixed. Gradually add the milk, mixing well. Stir in the vanilla extract. Line a metal strainer with a double thickness of cheesecloth. Strain the custard through the cheesecloth into the unbaked crust. Sprinkle with nutmeg. Bake for 40 to 45 minutes, or until a thin knife blade comes out clean when inserted into the custard halfway between the edge of the pan and the center of the custard. Cool completely on a wire rack. Refrigerate after the custard has cooled.

BUTTERNUT SQUASH PIE

Yield: 8 servings

*B*utternut squash can be used in much the same way as sweet potatoes or pumpkin. I remember my mother making mock candied yams with butternut squash and I couldn't tell the difference. As a lover of sweet potato custard, I must admit that this mildly spiced squash custard pie is equally as flavorful and delicious.

1½ cups puréed, cooked butternut squash
3 eggs
1 cup firmly packed light brown sugar
1 tablespoon all-purpose flour
¼ teaspoon ground cinnamon
⅛ teaspoon grated nutmeg
½ teaspoon salt
1 (9-inch) basic pie crust, unbaked (pages 140–141)

Preheat the oven to 425 degrees F.

In a large bowl, combine the squash, eggs, brown sugar, flour, cinnamon, nutmeg, and salt. Beat until well mixed. Pour into unbaked pie crust. Bake for 15 minutes. Reduce the heat to 325 degrees F. and bake for an additional 35 to 40 minutes, or until a thin knife blade comes out clean when inserted into the center of the pie. As the pie bakes, the filling will puff up, but as it cools it sinks down again. Cool on a rack before slicing. Serve with whipped cream, if desired.

APPLE CUSTARD PIE

Yield: about 8 servings

This is an updated version of a very old recipe. An easy-bake custard is filled with apples and raisins. The crust is lightly flavored with cinnamon. Any variety of apple works well with this custard.

CINNAMON CRUST

1½ cups all-purpose flour
1 teaspoon cinnamon
4 tablespoons chilled butter
¼ cup chilled shortening
3 to 4 tablespoons ice water

APPLE CUSTARD FILLING

3 egg yolks
¼ cup all-purpose flour
⅓ cup sugar
⅓ cup firmly packed light brown sugar
¼ cup milk
1 teaspoon vanilla extract
2 tablespoons butter or margarine, melted
2 cups chopped, cooked apples, well drained
½ cup raisins

MERINGUE

3 egg whites
¼ teaspoon cream of tartar
6 tablespoons sugar

Combine the flour and cinnamon in a large bowl. Stir to mix. Cut in the butter and shortening, using a food processor, pastry blender, or two knives, until the mixture resembles coarse cornmeal with a few lumps about the size of peas. Sprinkle the ice water over the mixture. Mix until the dough forms a ball. Shape into a disk about 1 inch thick. Refrigerate while preparing the filling.

Preheat the oven to 350 degrees F. Combine the egg yolks, flour, sugar, brown sugar, milk, vanilla, and butter. Mix well. Stir in the apples and raisins. Set aside.

On a lightly floured surface, roll the pastry to a circle about ⅛ inch thick. Fit the pastry into a 9-inch pie plate. Trim edge to about 1 inch larger than pie plate. Turn edge under and flute or press edge with a fork. Pour filling into pie shell. Bake for 30 to 35 minutes, or until a thin knife blade comes out clean when inserted into the center of the custard.

While the pie is baking, make the meringue. Beat the egg whites until foamy. Add the cream of tartar and continue beating until stiff peaks form and the sugar is completely dissolved. To test this, rub a small amount of the meringue between the finger and thumb. If it feels grainy, continue beating.

When the custard is cooked, smooth meringue over the top. Return to oven and bake for another 10 minutes, or until meringue is lightly browned.

SWEET POTATO PIE

Yield: 6 to 8 servings

*T*his is one dessert that I must stay away from when I am on a diet because I can't resist eating it. The blend of cooked sweet potatoes, butter, sugar, and just a hint of spice makes my taste buds tingle. The fact that this is an economical recipe and uses basic ingredients usually found in the kitchen pantry probably accounts for its popularity.

3 cups mashed, cooked sweet potatoes
¼ pound (1 stick) butter or margarine, softened at room temperature
⅔ cup sugar
⅓ cup firmly packed light brown sugar
1½ teaspoons vanilla extract
3 eggs
¼ teaspoon grated nutmeg
1 (9-inch) basic pie crust, unbaked (pages 140–141)

Preheat the oven to 400 degrees F.

Combine the sweet potatoes, butter, sugar, brown sugar, vanilla, eggs, and nutmeg. Mix well. Pour into unbaked pie crust. Bake for 10 minutes at 400 degrees F. Reduce the temperature immediately to 350 degrees F. and continue baking for an additional 35 minutes, or until a thin knife blade comes out clean when inserted into the center of the custard. Cool completely before slicing.

Cobblers

STRAWBERRY COBBLER

Yield: 8 to 10 servings

*T*he wonderful aroma of a strawberry cobbler baking in the oven is enough to make the mouth water. When I think of strawberry cobbler, Mother comes to mind because she could make the best strawberry cobbler in her favorite slightly bent cobbler pan.

FILLING

7 to 8 cups cut-up fresh strawberries
2 cups water
2 cups sugar
4 tablespoons all-purpose flour
12 tablespoons (1½ sticks) butter or margarine

CRUST

2½ cups all-purpose flour
⅔ cup shortening
4 to 6 tablespoons ice water
2 tablespoons butter or margarine, melted
1 teaspoon sugar

Preheat the oven to 350 degrees F.

Combine the strawberries and water in a 9x13x2-inch baking pan. Combine the sugar and flour in a medium bowl. Stir to mix. Sprinkle over the strawberries. Dot with butter.

To make the crust, combine the flour and shortening in the bowl of a food processor. Pulse until the mixture resembles coarse cornmeal with a few small lumps. Gradually add enough ice water for the mixture to pull together into a ball.

(continued)

On a lightly floured surface, roll the dough to a thickness of about ¼ inch. Cut into 1-inch strips. Make a latticed crust on top of the strawberry mixture. Brush with the melted butter. Sprinkle with sugar. Bake for 45 to 50 minutes, or until the crust is golden brown and the filling has thickened slightly.

NOTE: Instead of making the latticed crust, you can cover the entire top of the pie with pastry. Be sure to make some small slits in the dough to allow steam to escape.

FRESH BLACKBERRY COBBLER

Yield: 6 to 8 servings

*T*his is my favorite way to enjoy fresh blackberries. You will notice that the crust for this cobbler gives you a choice of liquid. Most of my cobbler crusts are made with ice water, but I remember my mother making a crust that was similar to biscuit dough, so I decided to try buttermilk in this crust. It's great. However, if you don't have any buttermilk on hand, don't make a special trip to the market because it only takes a few tablespoons for this recipe. Just use ice water instead. This cobbler is also good made with huckleberries or blueberries.

> *3½ to 4 cups fresh blackberries*
> *1 cup water*
> *1 cup sugar*
> *2 tablespoons all-purpose flour*
> *6 tablespoons butter or margarine*

CRUST
> *⅓ cup shortening*
> *1½ cups all-purpose flour*
> *3 to 4 tablespoons cold buttermilk or ice water*
> *1 tablespoon butter or margarine, melted*
> *1 teaspoon sugar*

Preheat the oven to 400 degrees F.

Pour the blackberries into a 2-quart casserole dish (about 8x8x2 inches) or a pan of equal size. Add the water. Combine the sugar and flour in a small bowl. Stir to mix. Sprinkle over berries. Dot with butter.

To make the crust, cut the shortening into the flour until the mixture resembles coarse cornmeal. This can be done quickly with a food processor but you can use a pastry blender or two knives. Add the buttermilk a tablespoon at a time and mix until the dough clings together and can be formed into a ball. On a lightly floured surface, roll the dough to a thickness of ⅛ to ¼ inch. Cut the dough to fit the top of the berry filling or cut into strips and make a lattice crust. Brush the crust with the melted butter. Sprinkle with sugar. Bake at 400 degrees F. for about 30 minutes. Reduce the temperature to 350 degrees F. Continue baking until the crust is golden brown and the juices have started to thicken. This will probably take an additional 15 to 20 minutes. As the pie cools, the juice will get thicker.

DEEP-DISH FRESH
PEACH COBBLER

Yield: 6 to 8 servings

This is a two-crust pie, but it is a bit unusual because one crust is in the middle of the pie. This crust becomes almost dumplinglike during baking. This is the way my mother made all her cobblers.

CRUST
⅔ cup shortening
2 cups all-purpose flour
4 to 5 tablespoons ice water

FILLING
6 cups peeled and sliced fresh peaches
1½ cups water
2 cups sugar
3 tablespoons all-purpose flour
¼ teaspoon ground cinnamon (optional)
12 tablespoons (1½ sticks) butter or margarine

Preheat the oven to 375 degrees F.

Make the crust by cutting the shortening into the flour until the mixture resembles coarse cornmeal. Gradually add the ice water until the mixture clings together and can be formed into a ball. Divide the dough in half. Roll each half to a square large enough to fit an 8x8x4-inch casserole dish or deep pan.

For the filling, put 3 cups of the peaches and 1 cup of the water in the casserole or pan. Combine the sugar with the flour and cinnamon. Stir to mix. Sprinkle half of this mixture over the peaches in the baking dish. Dot with half the butter. Cover with one square of dough. Make 2 or 3 small slits in the crust to allow steam to escape during baking. Bake for about 15 minutes, or until the crust no longer looks "doughy." Top with the remaining 3 cups peaches, ½ cup water, 1 cup sugar mixture, and 6 tablespoons butter. Place the remaining square of dough over the top. Cut several small slits in the top crust. If you like a buttery crust, brush the top with melted butter before baking. Bake for 40 to 45 minutes, or until the top crust is lightly browned and the filling is slightly thickened.

FAMILY REUNION
APPLE COBBLER

Yield: about 25 servings

*I*f you are attending a family reunion in the South and are asked to bring a covered dish, you had better make it big because there are some large Southern family trees and most Southerners love to eat! This cobbler would be a perfect "dish" to carry.

8 cups cooked or canned unsweetened apple slices, drained
3 cups water
2½ cups sugar
4 tablespoons all-purpose flour
1 teaspoon ground cinnamon
½ pound (2 sticks) butter or margarine

CRUST

2½ cups all-purpose flour
⅔ cup shortening
5 to 7 tablespoons ice water
2 tablespoons butter, melted
1 teaspoon sugar

Preheat the oven to 350 degrees F.

Combine the apples and water in a large baking pan or dish (about 11x15x3 inches). Combine the sugar, flour, and cinnamon in a small bowl. Stir to mix. Sprinkle over apples. Dot with butter.

To make the crust, combine the flour and shortening. Cut the shortening into the flour, using a food processor, two knives, or a pastry blender, until the mixture resembles coarse cornmeal. Add the ice water a tablespoon at a time until the mixture clings together and can be formed into a ball. On a lightly floured surface, roll the pastry to a rectangle large enough to fit over the top of the apples. There is no need to trim the edges. Just roll them forward and make a rim. Cut several small slits in the crust to allow steam to escape during baking. Brush with the melted butter. Sprinkle sugar over top. Bake 45 to 55 minutes, or until the crust is lightly browned and the filling is slightly thickened.

CANTALOUPE COBBLER

Yield: 6 to 8 servings

This doesn't taste nearly as strange as it might sound. In fact, it tastes almost like a peach cobbler. Quite flavorful!

4 cups peeled and sliced cantaloupe (slices should be about 1 inch thick)
1¼ cups water
1 cup sugar
2 tablespoons all-purpose flour
⅛ teaspoon ground cinnamon
5½ tablespoons butter or margarine

CRUST
1 cup all-purpose flour
¼ cup chilled shortening
2 to 3 tablespoons cold water

Preheat the oven to 375 degrees F.

Combine the cantaloupe and water in an 8x8x2-inch casserole or pan of approximate size. Combine the sugar, flour, and cinnamon. Stir to mix. Sprinkle over the cantaloupe. Dot with butter.

To make the crust, cut the shortening into the flour until the mixture resembles coarse cornmeal. Gradually add the cold water until the mixture clings together in a ball. On a lightly floured surface, roll the dough until it is large enough to cover the top of the fruit. Carefully place the crust on top of the filling. Cut several slits in the crust to allow steam to escape. Bake for 40 to 45 minutes, or until the crust is lightly browned and the filling is slightly thickened.

BERRY PATCH COBBLER ROLL

Yield: 8 to 10 servings

*T*his is one of the most unusual cobblers I have ever made or tasted. The berries are rolled up in a biscuit-type dough that is then cut into pinwheels. Any kind of berries can be substituted for the blueberries, and if you don't like pineapple juice, try another juice, milk, or water. This is an excellent recipe to use for kitchen experiments. An apple cobbler roll tastes wonderful. When I use apples, I like to use light brown sugar instead of the white granulated. This forms a caramel-like mixture. And, of course, I would use unsweetened apple juice for the liquid.

9½ tablespoons butter or margarine, melted
2¾ cups sugar
3 cups blueberries, fresh or frozen
2 tablespoons all-purpose flour
1 recipe Missouri Biscuits (page 208)
2½ cups unsweetened pineapple juice

Preheat the oven to 350 degrees F. Pour 8 tablespoons of the melted butter into a 9x13x2-inch baking pan. Pour 2 cups of the sugar over the butter.

In a large bowl, combine the remaining ¾ cup sugar, blueberries, and flour. Toss to coat the berries.

Knead the biscuit dough 5 or 6 times. Roll to a rectangle about 10x14 inches. Brush with the remaining 1½ tablespoons melted butter. Sprinkle the berry mixture over the butter. Press into dough slightly so that you can roll it more easily. Roll jelly-roll fashion from the 14-inch side. Pinch the edges of the dough to seal well. Cut into about 16 pinwheels. Place the pinwheels, cut side down, on top of the sugar in the pan. Pour the pineapple juice evenly over the top. Bake for 1 hour, until lightly browned and no longer doughy.

SWEET POTATO COBBLER

Yield: 8 to 10 servings

When I was growing up, the sweet potato was a staple in our kitchen. My mother could turn sweet potatoes into some of the best desserts I have ever tasted. My mouth waters every time I think about her candied "yams" with a slightly chewy but tender texture swimming in a pool of rich, caramel-flavored syrup. Sweet potato croquettes were her special children's treat. She always put a lot of butter, coconut, and raisins in the cooked, mashed "yams" and topped them with marshmallows. But my favorite is her sweet potato cobbler, mildly seasoned with spices and featuring a crispy pastry.

FILLING

6 cups (about 2 pounds) peeled and sliced sweet potatoes (potatoes should be
    cut crosswise into slices about ¼ inch thick)
2 cups sugar
3 tablespoons all-purpose flour
¼ teaspoon salt
½ teaspoon ground cinnamon
¼ teaspoon grated nutmeg
12 tablespoons (1½ sticks) butter or margarine

PASTRY

⅔ cup shortening
2 cups all-purpose flour
5 to 6 tablespoons ice water
2 tablespoons butter or margarine, melted
1 tablespoon sugar

In a large saucepan, combine the sweet potatoes with enough water to cover them. Boil until tender, about 15 minutes. The potatoes should be fork-tender, not mushy. Drain the potatoes but save the cooking liquid.

In a medium bowl, combine the sugar, flour, salt, cinnamon, and nutmeg. Stir to mix.

Preheat the oven to 400 degrees F. Butter a 9x13x2-inch baking pan. Pour the potatoes and 2 to 2½ cups of the cooking liquid into the prepared pan. Sprinkle with the sugar mixture. Dot with the butter.

To make the pastry, cut the shortening into the flour, using a food processor, pastry blender, or two knives, until the mixture resembles course cornmeal. Gradually add the water until the dough forms a ball.

On a lightly floured surface, roll the dough to a thickness of ⅛ to ¼ inch. Cover the potatoes completely with the crust or cut the pastry into 1-inch strips and make a lattice crust. If you choose the full crust, be sure to make several small slits in it so that the steam can escape during baking. Drizzle the crust with the melted butter. Sprinkle with the sugar. Bake 30 to 40 minutes, or until the crust is golden brown and the filling is bubbly and slightly thickened.

Baked Puddings

RICE PUDDING

Yield 8 servings

This is the perfect way to use leftover cooked rice. Just add a few basics (butter, milk, eggs, sugar, and vanilla) for a tasty and economical dessert.

3 cups cooked white rice
1 cup sugar
4 tablespoons butter or margarine, melted
3 eggs
2 cups milk
1 tablespoon vanilla extract

Preheat the oven to 350 degrees F. Butter an 8-inch-square baking dish that is at least 3 inches deep.

In a large bowl, combine the rice, sugar, and butter. Mix well. In a medium bowl, combine the eggs, milk, and vanilla. Beat with a fork until mixed. Add to the rice mixture. Mix well. Pour into baking dish. Bake for 40 to 45 minutes, or until pudding is set.

BUTTERMILK BREAD PUDDING

Yield: about 10 servings

*B*uttermilk is a staple in the Southern home and it adds an unusual and pleasing flavor to this pudding. I use cultured nonfat buttermilk, but you can use whole buttermilk in this pudding.

4 tablespoons butter or margarine
6 cups crumbled bread (can be French bread, biscuits, white bread, raisin
    bread, or a mixture of whatever breads you have on hand)
1 quart buttermilk
1 cup raisins
2 eggs, slightly beaten
1⅓ cups firmly packed, light brown sugar
1 tablespoon vanilla extract

BUTTER RUM SAUCE
¼ pound (1 stick) butter or margarine, softened at room temperature
1 cup sugar
1 egg yolk
¼ cup water
2 tablespoons rum

Preheat the oven to 350 degrees F. Melt the butter in a 9x13x2-inch baking pan.

Combine the bread, buttermilk, and raisins in a large bowl. Stir to mix. Set aside. In a medium bowl, combine the eggs, brown sugar, and vanilla. Mix until well blended. Add egg mixture to bread mixture. Mix well. Pour the pudding into the pan. Bake for 1 hour.

For the sauce, combine the butter, sugar, egg yolk, and water in a medium saucepan. Mix well. Cook over medium heat until the sugar has dissolved and the mixture begins to thicken. Remove from heat and stir in the rum. Serve warm with warm bread pudding.

BISCUIT PUDDING WITH CARAMEL APPLE SAUCE

Yield: about 20 servings

This is the old-fashioned version of bread pudding. Our Southern ancestors wouldn't dare throw away leftover biscuits because with a little milk, sugar, and eggs, these could be made into a tasty bread pudding. At serving time, they would sometimes pour milk over the baked pudding. At other times, it was served with a rich butter sauce. The caramel apple sauce is an updated version of a butter sauce.

6 tablespoons butter or margarine
6 cups coarsely crumbled biscuits, packed
1 quart milk
1 cup raisins
3 eggs
1½ cups sugar
2 teaspoons vanilla extract

CARAMEL APPLE SAUCE
¼ pound (1 stick) butter or margarine, softened at room temperature
⅔ cup firmly packed light brown sugar
1 egg yolk
2 tablespoons water
¼ cup unsweetened apple juice

Preheat the oven to 350 degrees F. Melt the butter in a 9x13x2-inch baking pan.

In a large bowl, combine the biscuits, milk, and raisins. Stir to mix. In a medium bowl, combine the eggs, sugar, and vanilla. Beat well. Add the egg mixture to the biscuit mixture. Mix well. Pour the pudding into the prepared pan. Bake for 1 hour.

For the sauce, combine the butter, brown sugar, egg yolk, and water in a medium saucepan. Mix well. Cook over medium-high heat, stirring constantly, until the sugar dissolves and the mixture thickens. Stir in the apple juice. Keep warm, over very low heat, then serve with warm bread pudding.

BREAD PUDDING WITH BOURBON SAUCE

Yield: 8 to 10 servings

*T*his is my version of the old-fashioned New Orleans-style bread pudding. The sauce is only faintly flavored with bourbon. I have found the amount of bourbon used in the true New Orleans recipe sometimes overpowers the delicate buttery flavor of the sauce.

4 tablespoons butter or margarine
6 cups coarsely crumbled French bread
1 quart milk
1 cup raisins
2 eggs
1 cup sugar
1 tablespoon vanilla extract

EASY BOURBON SAUCE
¼ pound (1 stick) butter or margarine, softened at room temperature
1 cup sugar
¼ cup water
1 egg yolk
2 tablespoons bourbon

Preheat the oven to 350 degrees F. Melt the butter in a 9x13x2-inch baking pan.

In a large bowl, combine the bread, milk, and raisins. Mix and set aside. In another bowl, combine the eggs, sugar, and vanilla. Beat with a fork until blended. Pour into the bread mixture and mix well. Pour the pudding mixture into the pan. Bake for 1 hour.

For the sauce, combine the butter, sugar, water, and egg yolk in a small saucepan. Mix well. Cook over medium heat until the sugar dissolves. Reduce heat to medium-low and continue cooking for about 3 minutes, or until the mixture starts to thicken. Remove from the heat and stir in the bourbon. Serve warm with bread pudding. Sauce can be reheated but do so over very low heat and do not allow the mixture to boil.

CHOCOLATE BREAD PUDDING
WITH AMARETTO SAUCE

Yield: about 10 servings

Years ago most Southern bakers would not dare use any type of alcoholic beverage in their recipes, but times are changing. With the understanding that the alcohol bakes away, leaving only a delightful flavor, more and more cooks in the South are using liqueurs and wines in cooking.

6 cups bread chunks, lightly packed
1 quart chocolate milk
⅔ cup sugar
2 tablespoons cocoa
2 eggs
4 tablespoons butter or margarine, melted
2 teaspoons vanilla extract
¾ cup chopped almonds

AMARETTO SAUCE
¼ pound (1 stick) butter or margarine, softened at room temperature
1 cup sugar
1 egg yolk
¼ cup water
2 tablespoons amaretto liqueur

Preheat the oven to 350 degrees F. Butter a 9x13x2-inch baking pan. Combine the bread chunks with the chocolate milk in a large bowl. Set aside.

Combine the sugar and cocoa in a small bowl. Stir to mix. Beat the eggs in a medium bowl. Gradually add the sugar mixture. Add the melted butter and vanilla extract. Beat well. Stir in the almonds. Add the bread mixture. Stir until well mixed. Pour into the prepared pan. Bake for 45 to 50 minutes.

For the sauce, combine the butter, sugar, and egg yolk in a small saucepan. Mix well. Add the water. Mix. Cook over medium heat until the sugar dissolves and the mixture is slightly thickened. Remove from the heat. Stir in the amaretto. Serve warm over the warm bread pudding.

TWIST O' LEMON BREAD PUDDING

Yield: about 10 servings

*T*his recipe shows how just a little touch of creativity can turn an ordinary dish into a new taste treat. My husband, Huey, loves anything lemon and if a lemon dessert appears on a restaurant menu, you can be fairly sure that it will find its way to our table. I simply added the lemon touch to my basic bread pudding and received raves from family and friends.

4 tablespoons butter or margarine
6 cups bread chunks, lightly packed
1 quart milk
2 large eggs
1 cup sugar
1 tablespoon pure lemon extract
2 teaspoons grated lemon peel
1 cup chopped pecans

LEMON BUTTER SAUCE

¼ pound (1 stick) butter or margarine, softened at room temperature
1 cup sugar
1 egg yolk
⅓ cup freshly squeezed lemon juice

Preheat the oven to 350 degrees F. Melt the butter in a 9x13x2-inch baking pan.

Combine the bread chunks and milk in a large bowl. Mix well. Set aside.

In another large bowl, beat the eggs and gradually add the sugar. Beat well. Stir in the lemon extract, lemon peel, and pecans. Mix well. Combine the bread mixture with the egg mixture. Mix well.

Pour the pudding mixture into the pan. Bake for about 1 hour, or until the mixture is set. Cool.

For the sauce, combine the butter and sugar in a heavy saucepan. Stir in the egg yolk, mixing well. Add the lemon juice. Mix. Place over medium heat. Cook until the sugar dissolves and the mixture is slightly thickened. Serve warm with cooled bread pudding.

PINEAPPLE BREAD PUDDING
WITH RUM SAUCE

Yield: about 12 servings

You get a taste of the tropics with this version of bread pudding. I like to use French bread because of the texture it gives to the pudding.

4 tablespoons butter or margarine
6 cups French bread chunks, lightly packed
1 quart milk
2 eggs
1 cup sugar
1 tablespoon vanilla extract
½ cup raisins
⅔ cup well-drained, crushed pineapple (reserve the juice)
½ cup coconut (canned or in plastic bags)
½ cup chopped pecans

PINEAPPLE RUM SAUCE
¼ pound (1 stick) butter or margarine, softened at room temperature
½ cup sugar
½ cup firmly packed light brown sugar
¼ cup pineapple juice
1 egg yolk
1 tablespoon light rum, or 1 teaspoon rum-flavored extract

Preheat the oven to 350 degrees F. Melt the butter in a 9x13x2-inch baking pan.

Combine the bread and milk in a large bowl. Stir to mix. In a medium bowl, combine the eggs, sugar, and vanilla extract. Beat until well blended. Stir in the raisins, crushed pineapple, coconut, and pecans. Add the bread mixture. Stir well. Pour the pudding mixture into the pan. Bake for 1 hour.

For the sauce, in a small saucepan, combine the softened butter, sugar, brown sugar, pineapple juice, and egg yolk. Stir until the egg yolk is well mixed with other ingredients. Cook over medium-high heat, stirring constantly, until sugar has dissolved. Reduce the heat to medium. Continue cooking for about 3 minutes, until the sauce has thickened. Stir continuously. Add the rum or extract. Serve warm with warm bread pudding.

BROWNIE FUDGE PUDDING

Yield: 8 servings

A rich fudge sauce forms as the pudding bakes. When it is served, spoon the sauce over the cakelike pudding. For a real dessert-lover's delicacy, serve it with whipped cream.

4 tablespoons butter or margarine, melted
1 cup sugar
1 teaspoon vanilla extract
1 cup all-purpose flour
3 tablespoons cocoa
1 teaspoon baking powder
¼ teaspoon salt
½ cup milk
⅔ cup chopped walnuts
1½ cups boiling water
1 cup heavy cream, sweetened and whipped (optional)

Preheat the oven to 350 degrees F.

In a large bowl, combine the butter, ½ cup of the sugar, the vanilla, flour, 1 tablespoon of the cocoa, the baking powder, salt, and milk. Mix well. Stir in walnuts.

In an 8- or 9-inch cake pan at least 2 inches deep, combine the remaining ½ cup sugar, 2 tablespoons cocoa, and the water. Mix well. Drop the brownie batter by tablespoonfuls into the cocoa mixture. Bake for about 30 minutes. Serve with whipped cream, if desired.

UNDERCOVER APPLE PUDDING CAKE

Yield: 6 servings

*A*delicious surprise is hidden beneath this lightly spiced cake. As it bakes, a rich caramel sauce forms on the bottom. In addition to being a super-easy dessert, there are no bowls to wash. The pudding cake is mixed, baked, and served in the same pan. Spoon it into a dessert bowl, top it with a scoop of vanilla ice cream, and you're in for a treat.

1 cup all-purpose flour
1½ cups firmly packed light brown sugar
1 teaspoon ground cinnamon
2 teaspoons baking powder
¼ teaspoon salt
½ cup milk
2 tablespoons oil
1 teaspoon vanilla extract
1 cup peeled, cored, chopped apple
1¼ cups hot unsweetened apple juice

Preheat the oven to 350 degrees F.

In an ungreased 9-inch cake pan (needs to be about 2 inches deep to prevent spillovers), combine the flour, ¾ cup of the brown sugar, the cinnamon, baking powder, and salt. Stir to mix. Add the milk, oil, and vanilla. Mix well. Stir in the apples. Spread the mixture evenly in the pan. Sprinkle the remaining ¾ cup of brown sugar over the top of the batter. Carefully pour the hot apple juice over the top. Bake for 40 to 45 minutes, or until a cakelike layer forms on top. Cool slightly before serving.

ORANGE DATE NUT PUDDING

Yield: 8 servings

Walnuts add a crunch to this rich date-filled pudding. It makes an elegant dessert when topped with whipped cream.

2 eggs
½ cup sugar
½ cup firmly packed light brown sugar
1 tablespoon all-purpose flour
¾ teaspoon baking soda
⅓ cup milk
3 tablespoons orange juice
1 cup chopped dates (not the sugared type)
½ cup chopped walnuts
1 cup heavy cream, sweetened and whipped (optional)

Preheat the oven to 300 degrees F. Butter a shallow 1½- to 2-quart casserole.

Combine the eggs, sugar, and brown sugar in a large bowl. Beat until mixed. Add the flour, baking soda, milk, and orange juice. Mix well. Stir in the dates and walnuts. Pour into prepared dish. Bake for 40 to 45 minutes. Serve warm with whipped cream, if desired.

Other Baked Desserts

•••••••••••••◗◉◖•••••••••••••

BAKED CUSTARD CUPS

Yield 8 servings

*T*hese individual custards have a flavor similar to the old-fashioned Southern egg custard, but the texture is smoother and creamier due to the larger amount of milk and the method of cooking in a water bath.

½ cup sugar
⅛ teaspoon salt
4 eggs
3 cups milk
1 teaspoon vanilla extract
Grated nutmeg (optional)

Preheat the oven to 325 degrees F.

In a large bowl, combine the sugar and salt. Stir to mix. Add the eggs and mix until blended. Gradually stir in the milk and the vanilla extract. Strain the custard into 8 (5-ounce) custard cups. Sprinkle with nutmeg, if desired. Place the cups in a shallow pan that is filled to a depth of about 1 inch with hot water. Bake for 35 to 40 minutes, or until a thin knife blade comes out clean when inserted near the center of the custard.

SAUCY CHOCOLATE
BUTTER ROLLS

....

Yield: 6 to 8 servings

*T*hese crunchy, buttery-tasting dessert rolls are made with easy yeast biscuit dough. After baking, the rolls are placed in a deep serving dish and covered with a creamy fudge sauce.

2 cups Southern Yeast Biscuit Dough (page 246)
3 tablespoons butter, melted

CHOCOLATE SAUCE

1½ cups sugar
1 tablespoon cocoa
¼ pound (1 stick) butter or margarine
½ cup milk
1 teaspoon vanilla extract

Preheat the oven to 450 degrees F. Lightly grease a baking sheet.

Spoon the dough onto a well-floured surface. Knead until no longer sticky. Roll to an 8x18-inch rectangle. Brush with the butter. Roll tightly, jelly-roll fashion, starting with the 18-inch side. Cut into about 16 slices. Place the slices cut side down on the baking sheet. Flatten slightly with the fingertips. Bake for 7 to 8 minutes, until lightly browned. Remove from pan. Cool on a rack. Place the rolls in a deep 2-quart casserole.

For the sauce, combine the sugar, cocoa, butter, and milk in a heavy saucepan. Cook over medium-heat until the sugar has dissolved and the mixture is smooth and slightly thickened. Remove from the heat. Stir in the vanilla. Don't overcook or the sauce could become grainy. Pour over the rolls.

NOTE: Any smooth commercial chocolate sauce can be substituted for the above.

Apple Dumplings

Yield: 4 servings

These tasty apple dumplings have two features that make them unusual. The pastry is made with apple juice and the dumplings are baked in a caramel mixture that forms a thick and creamy sauce.

APPLE PASTRY

¼ pound (1 stick) butter or margarine
1¾ cups all-purpose flour
3 to 5 tablespoons cold, unsweetened apple juice

FILLING

4 small (about 2½ inches in diameter) Granny Smith apples, peeled and
    cored
¼ cup sugar
⅛ teaspoon ground cinnamon

CARAMEL SAUCE

⅓ cup sugar
⅓ cup firmly packed light brown sugar
1 tablespoon butter or margarine
1 cup heavy cream

To make the pastry, cut the butter into the flour, using a food processor, two knives, or a pastry blender, until the mixture resembles coarse cornmeal. Gradually add the apple juice, mixing until the dough forms a ball. On a lightly floured surface, roll the pastry to a 12-inch square. Cut into four 6-inch squares.

Place an apple in the center of each square. Combine the sugar and cinnamon in a small bowl. Pour about 1 tablespoon of the sugar mixture into the center of each apple. Pull all four corners of the pastry to the top of the apple. Seal the edges by pinching together. Place the dumplings in an ungreased 9x13x2-inch baking pan.

Preheat the oven to 400 degrees F.

Make the sauce by combining the sugar, brown sugar, butter, and cream in a medium bowl. Mix well and pour around dumplings in pan. Bake for 30 to 35 minutes, basting with sauce about every 10 minutes. Dumplings are best served warm.

SWEET POTATO CUSTARD SQUARES

....

Yield: about 15 servings

*T*his triple-layer dessert features an easy "press in the pan" crust and a custardlike filling that is topped with a crispy praline crumble.

PRALINE CRUST AND CRUMBLE

2 cups all-purpose flour
1 cup firmly packed light brown sugar
12 tablespoons (1½ sticks) butter or margarine, softened at room temperature
1 cup chopped pecans

FILLING

3 cups mashed, cooked sweet potatoes
¼ pound (1 stick) butter or margarine, softened at room temperature
½ cup sugar
½ cup firmly packed light brown sugar
¼ teaspoon grated nutmeg
1 teaspoon vanilla extract
3 eggs

Preheat the oven to 350 degrees F. Grease a 9x13x2-inch baking pan.
Combine the crust ingredients in a large bowl and mix until crumbly. Reserve 1 cup for topping. Pat the remaining mixture into the bottom of the pan. Bake for 10 minutes.

(continued)

While the crust is baking, combine all the filling ingredients in a large bowl and mix well. Pour over the crust. Sprinkle the reserved 1 cup crumb mixture over the top of the filling. Bake for 35 to 40 minutes, or until the custard is set and the topping is lightly browned and crisp. Cool before slicing.

NOTE: This dessert freezes well, so save those leftovers.

Busy Baker Pies, Cobblers, and Puddings

PIES

COBBLERS

BAKED PUDDINGS

Pies

---◆━◉⬢◉━◆---

CHOCO-MINT PIE

Yield: 12 servings

The perfect one-word description for this easy-to-make pie is "refreshing." With the first bite, your mouth feels cool and your taste buds experience a delicious chocolate mint flavor. This pie is so rich that a small slice is all you will need. There is no crust because this easy and elegant dessert is actually a baked meringue filled with crumbled chocolate-covered mint wafers and crunchy walnuts. The mint wafers are the crisp cookie type, not the candy ones.

> *25 chocolate-covered mint wafers, coarsely crumbled (about 1⅔ cups)*
> *1 cup chopped walnuts*
> *3 egg whites*
> *¼ teaspoon baking powder*
> *⅔ cup sugar*
> *1 cup heavy cream, sweetened and whipped*

Preheat the oven to 350 degrees F. Butter a 9-inch pie plate or coat it with cooking spray.

Combine the crumbled wafers and walnuts in a small bowl. In a large mixing bowl, beat the egg whites until foamy. Add the baking powder and continue beating until soft peaks begin to form. Gradually add the sugar and beat until stiff peaks form. Gently fold in the wafer mixture. Pour into the pie plate and smooth the top. Bake for 20 minutes. Cool on a rack. When the pie is completely cool, cover with whipped cream. Refrigerate for an hour or two before serving.

POLKA DOT BROWNIE PIE

Yield: 8 to 10 servings

$\mathcal{T}$his could be called a chocoholic's dream pie. Topped with a scoop of ice cream, it becomes a heavenly treat.

²⁄₃ *cup sugar*
¹⁄₃ *cup firmly packed dark brown sugar*
¹⁄₄ *cup cocoa*
¹⁄₂ *cup all-purpose flour*
¹⁄₄ *pound (1 stick) butter or margarine, softened at room temperature*
2 eggs
1 teaspoon vanilla extract
¹⁄₈ *teaspoon salt*
¹⁄₂ *cup chopped pecans*
¹⁄₂ *cup chopped white chocolate (pieces should be about the size of chocolate chips)*
1 cup heavy cream, whipped (optional)

Preheat the oven to 325 degrees F. Grease a 9-inch pie plate.

Combine the sugar, brown sugar, cocoa, flour, butter, eggs, vanilla, and salt in a large bowl. Beat for 3 minutes. Stir in the pecans and white chocolate chunks. Pour into the prepared pie plate. Bake for 35 to 40 minutes, until wooden pick inserted into center of pie comes out barely moist. Don't overbake. Allow to cool on a rack. If desired, top with whipped cream or serve with vanilla ice cream.

LADY BALTIMORE PIE

Yield: about 8 servings

When I was growing up, at Christmastime Mother always baked her Lady Baltimore cake. I loved that divinity icing with candied fruits and nuts. Many years later when I was in a creative mood, I decided to see if I could capture that wonderful flavor in a quick-and-easy pie. When I took the first bite of my Lady Baltimore pie, I could almost taste Mom's special cake.

½ cup raisins
¼ cup unsweetened apple juice
½ cup chopped candied cherries
½ cup chopped candied pineapple
1 cup chopped pecans
1½ cups coarsely crushed tea cakes (page 125) or vanilla wafers
3 egg whites
½ teaspoon cream of tartar
1 cup sugar
1 teaspoon vanilla extract
1 cup heavy cream, sweetened and whipped

Combine the raisins and apple juice in a small bowl. Set aside for at least 15 minutes.

Preheat the oven to 350 degrees F. Butter a 9-inch pie pan.

In a medium bowl, combine the cherries, pineapple, pecans, crumbled tea cakes, and well-drained raisins. In a large mixing bowl, beat the egg whites until foamy. Add the cream of tartar. Continue beating until soft peaks begin to form. Gradually add the sugar, beating continuously until stiff peaks form. Add the vanilla. Mix well. Fold in the fruit mixture. Spoon into the prepared pan and smooth the top. Bake for 20 minutes. Remove from the oven and place on a rack to cool.

After the pie has cooled, top with whipped cream. Decorate with pecan halves, candied cherries, and candied pineapple. Refrigerate for at least 1 hour.

CHOCOLATE CHIP MYSTERY PIE

Yield: 8 servings

*T*he mystery is the combination of butter-type crackers, nuts, and miniature chocolate chips in a baked meringue. You get that chocolate chip cookie flavor in the airy texture of the meringue.

25 Ritz crackers, coarsely crumbled (about 1⅓ cups)
1 cup chopped pecans
½ cup miniature chocolate chips
3 egg whites
¼ teaspoon baking powder
1 cup sugar
1 teaspoon vanilla extract
1 cup heavy cream, sweetened and whipped

Preheat the oven to 350 degrees F. Butter a 9-inch pie plate or coat it with cooking spray.

Combine the crackers, pecans, and chips in a medium bowl. Stir to mix. In a large mixing bowl, beat the egg whites until foamy. Add the baking powder and beat until soft peaks form. Gradually add the sugar, beating until stiff peaks form. Add the vanilla. Beat well. Fold the cracker mixture into the egg whites. Pour into prepared pie plate and smooth the top. Bake for 20 minutes, until lightly browned and crispy on top. Cool on a rack, then refrigerate until ready to serve. Top with whipped cream.

Cobblers

Easy Cobbler

Yield: 6 to 8 servings

*W*ant cobbler for dessert but just don't have time to make the traditional one? This one's for you. The use of canned fruit and a quick stir-and-pour crust makes this the perfect cobbler for the busy baker.

4 tablespoons butter or margarine
1 (29 oz.) can sliced peaches (do not drain)
1 cup self-rising flour
1 cup sugar
1 cup peach nectar
1 cup heavy cream, whipped and sweetened to taste (optional)

Preheat the oven to 350 degrees F.

Melt the butter in a 10-inch cake pan. Pour the peaches into the pan with the melted butter. Combine the flour, sugar, and peach nectar in a small bowl. Beat until well mixed. Pour on top of the peaches. This batter doesn't have to cover the entire top of the pan because it will spread as it bakes. Also, don't worry if the batter sinks below the fruit because it will rise to the top as it bakes. Bake for about 45 minutes, or until golden brown on top. Serve with whipped cream or ice cream, if desired.

NOTE: If you want to bake the cobbler and don't have any peach nectar on hand, you can substitute milk or apple juice.

QUICK APPLE
CINNAMON COBBLER

Yield: 6 to 8 servings

A can of refrigerated cinnamon roll dough makes this cobbler unique. The cinnamon rolls are used instead of the traditional crust on top of an easy filling made with canned apple slices.

1 (20 oz.) can apple slices (not apple pie filling)
⅔ cup unsweetened apple juice
⅔ cup sugar
1½ tablespoons all-purpose flour
4 tablespoons butter or margarine
1 (8 count) can refrigerated cinnamon roll dough

Preheat the oven to 375 degrees F.

Pour the undrained apple slices and the apple juice into a 2-quart casserole dish or a pan of approximate size. Combine the sugar and flour in a small bowl. Stir to mix. Sprinkle over the apples. Dot with the butter. Place the unbaked cinnamon rolls, cinnamon side down, over the apples. Bake for 35 to 45 minutes, or until the apple filling starts to thicken. If the cinnamon rolls start to brown too quickly, cover loosely with aluminum foil.

NOTE: If you are one of those people who hates to waste anything, you can drizzle the glaze that is included in the can of cinnamon roll dough over the top of the baked cobbler.

Baked Puddings

————◦◦◦◦◦◦◦◦✦◦◦◦◦◦◦————

PINEAPPLE PUDDING SPOON-UP

··

Yield: 8 servings

This is definitely one of the easiest baked fruit puddings I have ever made. Basically, if you know how to use a mixer or food processor, you should have no problem with this dessert. All the ingredients are put into the bowl at one time and beaten for about a minute with an electric mixer (less with a food processor). Thirty-five minutes from start to finish. Quick, easy, and delicious!

4 eggs
½ cup self-rising flour
⅔ cup sugar
1 cup firmly packed light brown sugar
1 cup plain yogurt
1 (8 oz.) can crushed pineapple, undrained
4 tablespoons butter, melted
1 teaspoon vanilla extract
1 cup chopped pecans

Preheat the oven to 375 degrees F. Grease the bottom of a 9x13x2-inch baking pan.

If you are using an electric mixer, put all the ingredients in a large bowl and beat on high speed for about 1 minute. (With the food processor, stir in the pecans after the other ingredients are processed.) This is a very thin batter. Pour into pan. Bake for 30 minutes, until lightly browned and set. Cool slightly before serving. Spoon into dessert bowls. Top with ice cream or whipped cream, if desired.

HASTY BREAD PUDDING

Yield: about 6 servings

$\mathcal{M}$ost versions of bread pudding take about an hour to bake. This one takes about 30 minutes. There are only three ingredients in the pudding. Simple, quick, easy! Any kind of bread will do, such as leftover biscuits, sandwich bread, or French bread. You can vary the flavor by trying other pudding mixes, such as banana, lemon, or chocolate.

3½ to 4 cups crumbled bread (I like French bread because of the texture it gives the pudding)
1 (3 oz.) box vanilla pudding mix (the cook-and-serve kind, not the instant pudding mix)
3 cups milk

EASY BUTTER SAUCE
5½ tablespoons butter, softened at room temperature
⅔ cup sugar
1 egg yolk
2 tablespoons milk

Preheat the oven to 350 degrees F. Generously butter a 10x10x2-inch baking dish or pan of approximate size.

Combine the bread, pudding mix, and milk in a large bowl. Stir to mix well. Pour into buttered dish. Bake for about 30 minutes, or until the bread has absorbed the milk and the top of the pudding is light brown. During baking, the pudding will puff up, but as it cools it will sink down.

For the sauce, combine the softened butter, sugar, and egg yolk. Mix well. Stir in the milk. Cook over medium-high heat for 1 to 2 minutes, or until the mixture begins to thicken. This must be stirred constantly to prevent scorching. Serve with the bread pudding.

Breads

Southerners love breads almost as much as they love desserts. As soon as the bread comes from the oven, we like to have some butter close by to spread on this hot treat. Such quick breads as biscuits, corn bread, muffins, and loaves of nut bread have been more popular in the South than yeast breads.

In the past few years, the trend is changing just a little. More and more Southern bakers are venturing into yeast baking. Perhaps it is because home bakers are learning that baking with yeast is not as difficult as they might have once thought. Personally, working with yeast dough is a form of relaxation for me.

In addition to the plate of freshly baked biscuits on the breakfast table, it is nice to also have some homemade yeast sweet rolls or a slice of coffeecake to enjoy with a cup of coffee. Of course, this usually follows a big breakfast of biscuits, bacon, sausage, or ham served with eggs or gravy. Yes, and a bowl of buttered grits from time to time.

In the South, coffeecakes and sweet rolls are considered breads and therefore included in the bread chapter. For those who want coffeecake for breakfast but simply do not have the time to make it from scratch, there are many super-easy recipes among the Busy Baker breads. How about a few plum pockets made with canned biscuit dough? These will start your day off with a flavorful lift.

Bread Basket Favorites— Quick Breads

QUICK BREADS BAKED IN A LOAF PAN

OTHER QUICK BREADS

Biscuits & Corn Breads

SOUTHERN BISCUITS

Yield: 8 to 10 (2-inch) biscuits

*N*o bread says "Southern" quite like biscuits! For many years I have made biscuits the old-fashioned way: I squeeze them. This is the way my mother made biscuits and it took years for me to master the technique. Like Mother, I usually never measure the flour. A true Southern baker knows by the feel of the dough when enough flour has been added. Although most flour is presifted, I continue to sift the flour for these biscuits.

When Chef Nicholas Malgieri was visiting in our home, he asked that I call him before starting my morning biscuits. He wanted to see firsthand how they are made. Ordinarily, I would have been very nervous having an executive pastry chef watching over my shoulder, but Nick is a friend and I was thrilled that he was interested in my biscuits.

I filled my bowl with self-rising flour made from soft winter wheat, made a well in the center, and added the shortening (Mother used nothing but lard in her biscuits) and buttermilk. I started squeezing the mixture through my fingers, gradually working the flour into the shortening and buttermilk until I had a soft dough. Very little kneading is necessary. When the biscuits came from the oven, Nick examined them crumb by crumb and, much to my delight, gave them his stamp of approval.

2 to 2½ cups sifted, self-rising flour
½ cup lard (of course, you can substitute shortening)
1 cup buttermilk

Preheat the oven to 475 degrees F. Lightly grease a baking sheet.
Put the flour in a large mixing bowl. Make a well in the center. Add the

(continued)

lard and buttermilk. Start working the flour into the milk and shortening, squeezing the mixture through the fingers until a soft dough is formed. This will be a sticky dough. Lift the dough from the bowl and place on a well-floured surface. Sprinkle a little flour on top of the dough and start folding, gently kneading or pressing with the fingertips, and turning the dough until it is no longer sticky. Pat the dough to a thickness of about ½ inch. Cut with a 2-inch biscuit cutter. Place on the baking sheet. If you want the outside to be crispy, the biscuits should be placed about 1 inch apart. For a soft biscuit, place with edges touching. Bake for about 8 minutes, until lightly browned. Best served hot from the oven.

NOTE: Instead of cutting the biscuits, many Southern bakers prefer to pinch off small portions of dough to make balls about 1½ inches in diameter. These balls of dough are rolled in your palms, placed on the baking sheet, and pressed with the knuckles to flatten slightly.

FOOD PROCESSOR BISCUITS

Yield: 8 biscuits

These biscuits are not quite as light and fluffy as the old-fashioned kind, but they are tasty, quick, and easy. The recipe is written for the special soft-wheat flour used most often in the South. If you use a flour made from hard wheat, reduce the amount to 1½ cups.

2 cups self-rising flour
⅓ cup vegetable shortening
⅔ cup cultured nonfat buttermilk

Preheat the oven to 450 degrees F. Grease a 7-inch iron skillet or an 8-inch cake pan.

Combine all the ingredients in the bowl of a food processor fitted with the steel blade. Process for about 15 seconds. Remove the dough to a lightly floured surface. Gently knead 5 or 6 times. Pat or roll out to a thickness of ½ inch. Cut with a 2-inch biscuit cutter. Place the biscuits in the skillet. Bake for 8 to 10 minutes, until lightly browned.

NOTE: If you have any baked biscuits left over, don't throw them away. Coarsely crumble the biscuits, seal them in a freezer bag, and freeze them. Add to the bag each time you make biscuits. These can be used later for an old-fashioned bread pudding.

BEER BISCUITS

Yield: 10 to 12 biscuits

*B*eer adds just a slight taste of yeast to these crusty biscuits. They are crisp on the outside yet light and fluffy on the inside.

2 cups self-rising flour
⅓ cup vegetable shortening
⅔ cup beer (measured after the foam has gone down)

Preheat the oven to 450 degrees F. Grease a baking sheet.

Combine all the ingredients and mix well using a food processor fitted with the steel blade, or an electric mixer. This dough will be sticky and soft, but don't add extra flour. Place on a well-floured surface and sprinkle just a small amount of flour on top of the dough. Knead about 10 times.

Roll or pat to a thickness of about ½ inch. Cut with a 2-inch biscuit cutter. After cutting the biscuits, you can reroll the scrapes of dough, but do this only once. Place the biscuits about 2 inches apart on the baking sheet. Bake for about 10 minutes, until light golden brown.

MISSOURI BISCUITS

Yield: about 8 biscuits

*W*hen I was working at Peter Kump's New York Cooking School, I met Doris Eoff, a student from Missouri. Doris was attending school while her husband was working abroad. She had become so homesick that she was about to give up her classes and return to Missouri. I invited Doris to my apartment, hoping that I could help soothe those homesick blues. We both enjoy cooking and we spent some of the time together in the kitchen. I had very few cooking utensils so many times we had to improvise, which was really a lot of fun. I remember the first time we made biscuits. I had never had much luck making biscuits from all-purpose flour, which was all I could find in the supermarket. Without a recipe, Doris grabbed a bowl and stirred together some delicious biscuits with the all-purpose flour. These "Missouri biscuits" are the result of our fun in the kitchen.

> 1 to 2 tablespoons butter
> 2 cups all-purpose flour
> 1 tablespoon baking powder
> 1 teaspoon salt
> ⅓ cup vegetable oil
> ⅔ cup milk

Preheat the oven to 450 degrees F. Melt the butter in a 7-inch skillet.

In a large mixing bowl, sift together the flour, baking powder, and salt. Add the oil and milk. Beat until mixture clings together. Pinch off portions and roll into balls about 1½ inches in diameter. Flatten slightly. Place each biscuit in the butter and then turn it so that each side is coated. Bake for 8 to 10 minutes, until lightly browned. Serve hot.

SOUTHERN CORN BREAD

Yield: about 6 servings

Corn bread is almost as popular in the South as biscuits. It is the perfect flavor partner for dried beans, green beans, and turnip greens. Instead of serving stuffing with the Thanksgiving turkey, Southerners prefer corn bread dressing. For several weeks before the holidays, I save any leftover corn bread and freeze it to make dressing. Another way that Southerners enjoy their corn bread is crumbled in a glass of milk.

1⅓ cups self-rising cornmeal
½ cup self-rising flour
1 egg
⅔ cup milk
2 tablespoons vegetable oil

Preheat the oven to 450 degrees F. Generously grease a 7-inch iron skillet (or an 8-inch cake pan).

Combine the cornmeal and flour in a medium bowl. Stir to mix. Add the egg, milk, and oil. Mix well. Pour into the skillet. Bake for 18 to 20 minutes, until golden brown. Invert onto a serving plate. Cut into 6 to 8 portions and slide a fork or knife under the cut portions to prevent soggy bottoms.

CRACKLING CORN BREAD

Yield: about 6 servings

A vision of hog-killing time comes to mind when I think about cracklings. I had a bachelor uncle who lived on a farm. When the first cold spell came along, Uncle Mack would kill a hog. Mother and Daddy would make the sausage, cure the hams, and make the lard. After Mother had made the lard, she would put the small remnants of fat into a cast-iron skillet that she placed in the oven. When the fat became crisp, she would put it into some type of press and squeeze out as much grease as she could. What was left was called "cracklings." These crispy tidbits of fat add a unique flavor to corn bread.

Cracklings are available in some supermarkets, but you can also make your own. One half pound of pork fat will render about ½ cup cracklings. To make the cracklings, cut the pork fat into ¼-inch cubes. Cook in a heavy skillet (preferably iron) over medium-high heat until the fat pieces become crisp and light brown. Pour off excess grease as it accumulates.

2 tablespoons oil
1⅓ cups cornmeal
½ cup plus 2 tablespoons self-rising flour
½ cup cracklings
1 egg
¾ cup milk

Preheat the oven to 475 degrees F.

Pour the oil into a 7-inch iron skillet (or 8-inch cake pan). Place the skillet in the oven to heat the oil. In a large bowl, combine the cornmeal, flour, cracklings, egg, and milk. Mix well. Pour into the skillet. Bake for 15 to 20 minutes, until browned. Turn out of skillet onto a serving plate. Cut into wedges and place a fork or knife under the pieces to prevent soggy bottoms.

Muffins

BLUEBERRY LEMON MUFFINS

Yield: 12 (2½-inch) muffins

There is just enough lemon in these tasty muffins to enhance the flavor of the blueberries. The high-fat content in the heavy cream eliminates the need for butter or oil.

2 cups self-rising flour
⅔ cup sugar
1 teaspoon grated lemon peel
1 cup fresh blueberries, washed and drained
2 eggs
1 tablespoon freshly squeezed lemon juice
1 teaspoon vanilla extract
½ cup heavy cream

Preheat the oven to 400 degrees F. Grease a 12-cup (⅓ cup capacity each) muffin tin.

In a large bowl, combine the flour, sugar, and lemon peel. Stir to mix. Remove ¼ cup of the flour mixture and coat the blueberries with it.

In a medium bowl, beat together the eggs, lemon juice, vanilla extract, and heavy cream. Add the flour mixture and stir just until the dry ingredients are moistened. Do not overmix. Stir in the blueberries. Fill muffin cups about two thirds full. Bake for 18 to 20 minutes, or until a wooden pick comes out clean when inserted into the center of a muffin. Remove muffins from pan immediately. Serve warm with butter. They are also good cooled.

NOTE: If you use all-purpose flour, add 1 tablespoon baking powder and ¾ teaspoon salt.

APPLE MYSTERY MUFFINS

Yield: 12 (2½-inch) muffins

*T*hese muffins have a cakelike texture. When I developed my first version of the muffins about 20 years ago, I used water and saltines for making the mock applesauce. Later, when I tried the apple juice and butter-type crackers, I like them much better because the muffins were more flavorful.

½ cup unsweetened apple juice
1 cup firmly packed light brown sugar
1 teaspoon ground cinnamon
¾ cup coarsely crumbled Ritz crackers (about 14 crackers)
½ cup raisins
1½ cups all-purpose flour
1 teaspoon baking soda
⅛ teaspoon salt
¼ pound butter (1 stick) butter, softened at room temperature
1 egg

APPLE GLAZE

1 cup confectioners' sugar
1½ tablespoons apple juice

Preheat the oven to 350 degrees F. Grease a 12-cup (⅓ cup capacity each) muffin tin.

Combine the apple juice, ½ cup of the brown sugar, and cinnamon in a small saucepan. Bring to a boil. Add the crackers and reduce heat to medium. Cook until the mixture is about the consistency of applesauce. Remove from the heat. Stir in the raisins.

Combine the flour, baking soda, salt, butter, egg, and remaining ½ cup brown sugar in a large mixing bowl. Beat until smooth. Stir in the cracker mixture. Fill the muffin cups two thirds full. Bake for 18 to 20 minutes, or until a wooden pick comes out clean when inserted into the center of one of the muffins. Remove the muffins from the pan and place on a rack to cool.

To make the glaze, combine and beat the sugar and juice until smooth. Drizzle over the cooled muffins.

APPLE CHEESE MUFFINS

Yield: 12 (2½-inch) muffins

One of the foods that I remember from my days as a high school lunchroom helper is apple pie with a wedge of cheese on top. This flavor combination has remained a favorite since those school days so it is not unusual that I would choose to add some Cheddar to my apple muffins.

2 cups all-purpose flour
3 teaspoons baking powder
¾ teaspoon ground cinnamon
¼ teaspoon salt
⅓ cup vegetable oil
1 egg
½ cup milk
⅓ cup honey
1 cup finely chopped peeled apple
½ cup shredded or grated Cheddar cheese
½ cup chopped pecans

GLAZE

1 cup confectioners' sugar
1 to 1½ tablespoons unsweetened apple juice or milk

Preheat the oven to 375 degrees F. Grease 12 muffin cups (⅓ cup capacity each).

In a large mixing bowl, combine the flour, baking powder, cinnamon, and salt. Stir to mix. Add the oil, egg, milk, and honey. Mix just until well blended. Stir in the apple, cheese, and pecans. Fill the muffin cups about two thirds full. Bake for 18 to 20 minutes, or until a wooden pick comes out clean when inserted into the center of a muffin.

For the glaze, combine the confectioners' sugar and apple juice in a small bowl. Beat until smooth. Drizzle over tops of the cooled muffins.

HUSH PUFFINS

Yield: about 8 (2½-inch) muffins

*T*hese are a cross between hush puppies and corn muffins. In the South, when there's a fish fry, there's hush puppies. But even Southerners are beginning to cut back on fried foods. These muffins are a good stand-in for hush puppies. They are similar in flavor but are not greasy like their fried cousins.

1 cup cornmeal
⅓ cup all-purpose flour
½ teaspoon baking soda
¼ teaspoon salt
⅓ cup finely chopped onion
1 egg
½ cup buttermilk
¼ cup oil

Preheat the oven to 450 degrees F. Generously grease 8 muffin cups (⅓ cup capacity each). Combine all the ingredients in a medium bowl. Mix well. Spoon into muffin cups, filling about two thirds full. Bake for 15 to 18 minutes. Remove from the muffin pan immediately. Serve warm.

CINNAMON CARROT MUFFINS

Yield: about 16 muffins

*D*elightful lunch box treat and, best of all, the children won't even realize that they are eating a wholesome treat.

2/3 cup pineapple juice
1/2 cup firmly packed light brown sugar
1 teaspoon ground cinnamon
1 cup coarsely crumbled wheat crackers
1 cup raisins
1/3 cup sugar
1 2/3 cups self-rising flour
1/4 pound (1 stick) butter or margarine, softened at room temperature
1 egg
3 tablespoons grated carrots
1/4 cup well-drained crushed pineapple
1/2 cup chopped pecans

PINEAPPLE GLAZE

1 cup confectioners' sugar
1 1/2 to 2 tablespoons pineapple juice

Preheat the oven to 350 degrees F.

In a small saucepan, combine the pineapple juice, brown sugar, cinnamon, and crackers. Cook over medium heat until the mixture is the consistency of applesauce. Remove from the heat and stir in the raisins.

Combine the sugar, flour, butter, egg, carrots, and pineapple in a large bowl. Mix well. Stir in the cracker mixture and the pecans.

Line muffin tins with paper liners. Spoon the batter into the cups, filling each about two thirds full. Bake for 18 to 20 minutes, or until a wooden pick inserted into the center comes out clean. Remove from tins. Cool on a rack.

To make the glaze, combine the confectioners' sugar and pineapple juice in a small bowl. Beat until smooth. Drizzle over the cooled muffins.

NOTE: When using all-purpose flour, add 1 teaspoon baking soda and 1/8 teaspoon salt.

HUCKLEBERRY HONEY MUFFINS

Yield: 12 (2½-inch) muffins

When I was a youngster, I always looked forward to huckleberry time. My favorite way to enjoy huckleberries was to eat them fresh from the picking. Huckleberries are best in these muffins because they are smaller than blueberries and their wonderful flavor is distributed more evenly through the muffins. Of course, if you don't have any wild huckleberries, their cultivated cousin, the blueberry, will do.

1¾ cups all-purpose flour
2½ teaspoons baking powder
½ teaspoon salt
½ cup sugar
1 cup fresh huckleberries
5½ tablespoons butter, melted
¼ cup honey
1 egg
½ cup milk

Preheat the oven to 400 degrees F. Grease a 12-cup muffin tin (⅓ cup capacity each).

Combine the flour, baking powder, salt, and sugar in a large bowl. Stir to mix. Remove ⅓ cup of the flour mixture and coat the huckleberries with it.

In a medium bowl, beat together the butter, honey, egg, and milk. Add to the dry ingredients. Mix just until the dry ingredients are moistened. Do not overmix. Gently stir in the huckleberries. Fill muffin cups two thirds full. Bake for about 18 minutes, or until a wooden pick inserted into the center of a muffin comes out clean. Remove the muffins from the pan immediately. Best served hot from the oven—with butter, of course!

BRAN MUFFINS FOR A BUNCH

Yield: 6 to 7 dozen (2½-inch) muffins

*W*hen making these muffins, be sure you have an extra large bowl for mixing. They are best if the batter is refrigerated at least 8 hours. It can be kept in the refrigerator for up to 6 weeks and used as needed.

1 (15 oz.) box raisin bran
3 cups whole wheat flour
2 cups all-purpose flour
½ cup sugar
⅔ cup firmly packed light brown sugar
5 teaspoons baking soda
1 teaspoon salt
1 teaspoon ground cinnamon
4 eggs
1 cup vegetable oil
4 cups buttermilk

Combine all the ingredients in a very large bowl. Mix well. Cover and refrigerate. When ready to bake, remove as much batter as you need and return remainder to refrigerator.

Preheat the oven to 375 degrees F. Grease as many muffin pans as needed. Fill muffin cups about two thirds full. Bake for 18 to 20 minutes, or until a wooden pick inserted into the center comes out clean. Best served warm with butter.

PEACHES AND CREAM MUFFINS

Yield: 12 (2½-inch) muffins

*S*outherners love peaches . . . fresh, canned, preserves, or jam. Tasty peach preserves blend with sour cream to make these muffins moist and delicious. If you have some homemade peach preserves, by all means use it. Otherwise, store-bought will be okay.

> *2 cups all-purpose flour*
> *¼ cup sugar*
> *¼ cup firmly packed brown sugar*
> *1 teaspoon baking soda*
> *⅛ teaspoon salt*
> *2 eggs*
> *½ cup sour cream*
> *½ cup peach preserves*
> *⅓ cup vegetable oil*

Preheat the oven to 400 degrees F. Grease a 12-cup muffin tin (⅓ cup capacity each).

In a large bowl, combine the flour, sugar, brown sugar, baking soda, and salt. Stir to mix.

In a medium bowl, beat together the eggs, sour cream, preserves, and oil. Add to the dry ingredients and stir only until the dry ingredients are moistened. Do not overmix. Fill the muffin cups about two thirds full. Bake for 20 to 25 minutes, or until a wooden pick inserted into the center of a muffin comes out clean. Remove muffins from pan immediately. Serve warm with butter.

FIG MUFFINS

Yield: 12 (2½-inch) muffins

I adore figs picked fresh from the tree, but figs were not in season when I decided to make these muffins so I used dried figs.

2 tablespoons butter or margarine, melted
1 egg
1 cup buttermilk
⅓ cup firmly packed light brown sugar
1½ cups all-purpose flour
1½ teaspoons baking powder
½ teaspoon baking soda
¼ teaspoon salt
⅔ cup finely chopped dried figs
½ cup chopped pecans

Preheat the oven to 425 degrees F. Grease a 12-cup muffin pan (⅓ cup capacity each).

Combine the melted butter, egg, and buttermilk in a large bowl. Mix well.

Combine the brown sugar, flour, baking powder, baking soda, and salt. Stir to mix. Add the flour mixture to the liquid ingredients, mixing only until dry ingredients are moistened. Do not overmix. Stir in the figs and pecans. Spoon into muffin cups, filling about two thirds full. Bake for 15 to 20 minutes, or until a wooden pick comes out clean when inserted into the center of one of the muffins. Best served warm with butter.

Quick Breads Baked in a Loaf Pan

━━━━•➤)✪(◄•━━━━

ZUCCHINI CARROT BREAD

Yield: about 10 servings

This is one of my favorite quick breads because it is as pleasing to the eye and nose as it is to the palate. When you cut into the loaf, you see tiny "freckles" of orange and green. This sweet bread has a crunchy crust and a tender crumb.

2 cups all-purpose flour
1 cup firmly packed light brown sugar
2 teaspoons baking powder
⅛ teaspoon ground cloves
⅛ teaspoon grated nutmeg
¼ teaspoon ground cinnamon
⅛ teaspoon salt
½ cup vegetable oil
2 eggs
⅔ cup finely shredded zucchini
⅔ cup finely shredded carrots
¾ teaspoon vanilla extract

Preheat the oven to 375 degrees F. Grease a 9x5x3-inch loaf pan.

In a medium bowl, combine the flour, brown sugar, baking powder, spices, and salt. Stir to mix.

In a large bowl, beat together the oil and eggs. Stir in the zucchini, carrots, and vanilla. Add the flour mixture and beat until smooth. Pour into the loaf pan. Bake for 45 to 50 minutes, or until a wooden pick comes out clean when inserted into the center of the loaf. Remove from the pan immediately. Best served warm with butter.

SWEET POTATO BREAD

Yield: about 10 servings

*S*weet potato bread has been a Southern favorite for many years. In fact, just about anything made with sweet potatoes will delight the Southern palate. People in the South also tend to use more sweetener than cooks in other parts of the country. This recipe is no exception. It is indeed sweeter than your usual quick bread and could almost be served as dessert. The recipe is old, but the pineapple and ginger combination is my little contribution to an already tasty bread.

2 cups all-purpose flour
1 teaspoon baking soda
¼ teaspoon baking powder
¼ teaspoon salt
½ teaspoon ground ginger
½ teaspoon ground cinnamon
¼ pound (1 stick) butter, softened at room temperature
½ cup sugar
½ cup firmly packed light brown sugar
2 eggs
1 teaspoon vanilla extract
1 cup mashed cooked sweet potatoes
½ cup drained crushed pineapple
2 tablespoons milk
½ cup chopped pecans or walnuts

Preheat the oven to 350 degrees F. Grease and lightly flour a 9x5x3-inch loaf pan.

Combine the flour, baking soda, baking powder, salt, ginger, and cinnamon in a medium bowl.

Combine the softened butter, sugar, brown sugar, eggs, and vanilla in a large mixing bowl. Beat until well blended. Add the sweet potatoes, pineapple, flour mixture, and milk. Mix well. Stir in the chopped nuts. Pour into prepared pan. Bake for about 1 hour, or until a wooden pick inserted into the center of the loaf comes out clean. Remove from the pan immediately. Cool on a rack.

BANANA WALNUT BREAD

Yield: about 10 servings

When someone mentions quick bread, I automatically think of banana nut bread, though there are many other wonderful breads that fall into this category. When I was growing up, banana nut bread was about the only sweet quick bread that I remember eating.

¼ pound (1 stick) butter or margarine, softened at room temperature
½ cup sugar
½ cup firmly packed light brown sugar
2 eggs
1 teaspoon vanilla extract
1¼ cups mashed banana (about 3 small bananas)
2 cups all-purpose flour
1 teaspoon baking soda
½ teaspoon salt
½ cup chopped walnuts

Preheat the oven to 350 degrees F. Grease and lightly flour a 9x5x3-inch loaf pan.

Combine the butter, sugar, and brown sugar in a large mixing bowl. Beat until well blended. Add the eggs, vanilla extract, and bananas. Beat just until mixed.

Combine the flour, baking soda, and salt in a medium bowl. Stir to mix. Gradually add the flour mixture to the batter. Mix just until blended. Stir in the walnuts. Pour into prepared pan. Bake for 40 to 50 minutes, or until a wooden pick inserted into the center of the loaf comes out clean. Remove from the pan immediately. Cool on a rack.

BLACK WALNUT BREAD

Yield: about 10 servings

*A*ll that is needed when this aromatic bread comes from the oven is butter. It makes a wonderful quick breakfast bread.

2 cups all-purpose flour
2 teaspoons baking powder
¼ teaspoon salt
⅔ cup sugar
¼ pound (1 stick) butter or margarine, melted
2 eggs
⅔ cup milk
2 teaspoons vanilla extract
1 cup chopped black walnuts

Preheat the oven to 350 degrees F. Grease a 9x5x3-inch loaf pan.

In a medium bowl, combine the flour, baking powder, salt, and sugar. Stir to mix.

In a large bowl, combine the butter, eggs, milk, and vanilla extract. Beat well. Gradually add the flour mixture, beating well. Stir in the black walnuts. Pour into prepared pan. Bake for 45 to 50 minutes, or until a wooden pick inserted into the center of the loaf comes out clean. Remove from pan immediately.

BEER CHEESE BREAD

Yield: about 8 servings

This recipe is an adaptation of one given to me by a friend several years ago. After reading the recipe, I decided that a little Cheddar might make it better. I will always remember the first time I made the beer cheese bread because I couldn't get it out of the pan. Everywhere the cheese peeked through the batter, it stuck to the pan. The second time I made the bread, I greased the pan and sprinkled it generously with dry bread crumbs. Problem solved! This easy-to-make bread uses only six simple ingredients. As the bread bakes, a wonderful yeastlike smell permeates the air, although there is no yeast in the recipe. Serve it warm with butter.

2 tablespoons fine dry bread crumbs
3 cups self-rising flour
2 tablespoons sugar
1 cup shredded Cheddar cheese
12 ounces beer
1 to 2 tablespoons butter, melted

Preheat the oven to 350 degrees F. Grease a 9x5x3-inch loaf pan and sprinkle it generously with the dry bread crumbs. Shake out any excess crumbs.

In a large mixing bowl, combine the flour, sugar, and cheese. Stir to mix. Add the beer and mix well. Pour the stiff batter into the prepared pan. Bake for 45 minutes. Brush with the melted butter. Bake for an additional 10 to 15 minutes, until golden brown. Serve warm, with butter.

PEAR BREAD

Yield: 10 servings

*T*his bread is made with a butterscotch "flour." A food processor is needed to distribute the smooth butterscotch flavor throughout the bread. It is a beautiful, moist, and delicious bread that could be served as dessert.

2 cups all-purpose flour
1 (6 oz.) package butterscotch morsels
½ teaspoon baking powder
¼ teaspoon baking soda
¼ teaspoon salt
⅓ cup sugar
2 eggs
2 tablespoons butter, softened at room temperature
1 cup sour cream
1 teaspoon vanilla extract
1 cup peeled and finely chopped fresh firm pears

Preheat the oven to 350 degrees F. Grease and lightly flour a 9x5x3-inch loaf pan.

In the bowl of a food processor fitted with the steel blade, combine the flour and butterscotch morsels. Process until the morsels are almost as fine as the flour. Add the baking powder, baking soda, salt, and sugar. Pulse until mixed. Add the eggs, butter, sour cream, and vanilla. Process until well blended. Remove the blade. Stir in the pears. Pour into the prepared pan. Bake for 50 to 60 minutes, or until a wooden pick inserted into the center of the loaf comes out clean. Cool in the pan about 3 minutes. Invert onto a rack to cool completely.

Other Quick Breads

PROCESSOR CRACKER BREAD

Yield: 6 to 8 servings

This thin and crisp bread is the perfect "go-with" for soup or salad. It is also great eaten plain as a snack. A food processor is needed for this cracker bread.

2⅓ cups all-purpose flour
½ teaspoon salt
½ teaspoon sugar
1 egg
2 tablespoons butter or margarine
½ cup milk
3 tablespoons sesame seeds
1 tablespoon poppy seeds
1 tablespoon caraway seeds

Preheat the oven to 475 degrees F. Flour a large (at least 10x15 inch) baking sheet.

In the bowl of a food processor fitted with the steel blade, combine the flour, salt, sugar, egg, butter, and milk. Process until the dough forms a ball. Let stand for at least 1 hour. On a lightly floured surface, roll the dough very thin (about ⅛ inch thick). Combine the seeds in a small bowl. Sprinkle the seeds over the dough. Roll the dough again just enough to push the seeds into the dough. Place on the large floured baking sheet.

Place a pan of hot water on the shelf beneath the one holding the bread. Bake for 5 minutes. Remove the pan of water. Reduce the temperature to 350 degrees. Bake an additional 20 minutes, until the bread is golden brown. Remove from the pan and place on a rack to cool. When completely cooled, break the bread into irregular pieces.

APPLE BRAN COFFEECAKE

Yield: about 12 servings

*T*his fiber-rich cake is pleasing even to those who dislike bran.

1½ cups All-Bran
1 cup butterscotch morsels
½ cup chopped pecans
1¼ cups all-purpose flour
½ teaspoon baking powder
¾ teaspoon baking soda
½ cup sugar
½ cup firmly packed light brown sugar
2 eggs
¼ pound (1 stick) butter or margarine, softened at room temperature
1 cup sour cream
1 cup peeled and grated apples (I use red Delicious for this coffeecake)

GLAZE

1 cup confectioners' sugar
1½ to 2 tablespoons milk or apple juice
¼ teaspoon vanilla extract

Preheat the oven to 350 degrees F. Grease a 9x13x2-inch baking pan.

Combine the All-Bran and the butterscotch morsels in the bowl of a food processor fitted with the steel blade. Process until the mixture is fine but not powdery. Pour this mixture into a medium bowl. Stir in the pecans. Reserve ¾ cup of this mixture for the streusel.

Combine the flour, baking powder, baking soda, sugar, brown sugar, eggs, butter, and sour cream in a large mixing bowl. Beat until well blended. Stir in the bran mixture (except for the reserved ¾ cup) and the apples. Pour the batter into the prepared pan. Sprinkle the top with the reserved bran mixture. Bake for 30 to 35 minutes, or until a wooden pick comes out clean when inserted into the center of the coffeecake. Cool in the pan for about 10 minutes on a cake rack.

To make the glaze, combine all glaze ingredients and beat until smooth. Drizzle over warm coffeecake.

PEPPER CASSEROLE BREAD

Yield: 6 to 8 servings

*T*he aroma coming from the oven as this bread bakes is enough to send your taste buds into a tizzy. I'm not exactly sure what a tizzy is but I remember hearing it for most of my life. I guess it's just Southern slang for a whirlwind of enjoyment. The texture is more like a cake than a bread.

2 tablespoons seasoned dry bread crumbs
1½ cups all-purpose flour
2 teaspoons baking powder
¼ teaspoon salt
½ teaspoon baking soda
½ cup cornmeal
2 tablespoons grated Parmesan cheese
1 cup sour cream
1 egg
⅓ cup vegetable oil
⅔ cup finely chopped bell pepper (a combination of red and green bell
    peppers gives it a festive appearance)
2 tablespoons finely chopped green onions

Preheat the oven to 400 degrees F. Generously grease a 1½- to 2-quart casserole dish or an 8-inch round cake pan that is at least 2 inches deep. (If you use a metal cake pan, increase the temperature to 425 degrees F.) Coat the casserole or pan with the bread crumbs. Shake out any excess crumbs.

Combine the flour, baking powder, salt, baking soda, cornmeal, and Parmesan cheese in a large mixing bowl. Stir to mix. Add the sour cream, egg, and oil. Beat until well mixed. Stir in the bell pepper and onion. Pour into the prepared casserole or cake pan. Bake for about 20 minutes, until golden brown. Turn out of the pan immediately. Best served warm with butter.

Memorable Yeast Breads

DINNER ROLLS

Yield: about 18 large rolls

*A*t least once a year, Southern biscuits are put aside for homemade yeast rolls. Each Thanksgiving our home is the setting for a big family dinner. Usually seated around our table are our daughters and their families and my mother-in-law. The homemade rolls are such a big hit that my mother-in-law suggested that we sometimes serve only a large basket of the rolls and some butter for Thanksgiving instead of the large traditional meal. Not a bad idea because I could enjoy a meal of rolls and butter.

1 teaspoon plus 2 tablespoons sugar
¼ cup warm water
1 package (¼ oz.) active dry yeast
1 cup milk
1 egg
¼ cup shortening, melted
1 teaspoon salt
3 to 4 cups all-purpose flour

In a small bowl, combine the 1 teaspoon sugar, water, and yeast. Stir to mix. Set aside until the mixture becomes bubbly.

In a large mixing bowl, combine the remaining 2 tablespoons sugar, milk, egg, melted shortening, and salt. Beat to mix. Add 1 cup of the flour and the yeast mixture. Mix well. Gradually add the remaining flour until a moderately firm dough is formed. Turn the dough onto a lightly floured surface and knead for 3 to 5 minutes, until the dough is no longer sticky. Place in a large oiled bowl and turn the dough so that all surfaces are oiled. Cover with a clean dish towel and allow to rise in a warm place until doubled. This takes about 1 hour.

Punch down the dough and cover with a towel. Allow the dough to rest for about 10 minutes. Pinch off portions about the size of a large walnut. Roll into balls (or shape as desired) and place on a greased baking sheet. Cover with the towel and set in a warm place until doubled. This usually takes about 45 minutes.

Preheat the oven to 400 degrees F. Bake for 12 to 15 minutes, until lightly browned. Serve warm with butter.

WHITE BREAD

Yield: 2 loaves

*I*t was many years after I started baking with yeast that I finally decided to try my hand at making a loaf of white bread. I don't know why, but previously just the thought of it made me nervous. But I soon learned that baking a beautiful and tasty loaf of white bread can be easy. I was thrilled when I cut into my first loaf. It was a delight to the eyes and to the palate. Most of my yeast breads are made with all-purpose flour, but for this special bread I use bread flour.

¼ cup warm water
1 teaspoon plus 1½ tablespoons sugar
1 (¼ oz.) package dry yeast
2 teaspoons salt
2 cups milk, at room temperature
2 tablespoons shortening, melted
5 to 6 cups bread flour

Combine the warm water and 1 teaspoon sugar in a small bowl. Add yeast. Stir to mix. Set aside until the mixture becomes bubbly.

In a large bowl, combine the remaining 1½ tablespoons sugar, salt, milk, and melted shortening. Mix well. Add 1 cup of the flour and the yeast mixture. Mix well. Add another cup of flour and whisk until the mixture is smooth. (This can also be done with an electric mixer.) Continue adding flour until the dough is moderately stiff. Turn out onto a lightly floured surface. Knead until the dough is smooth and elastic. The kneading time should be 8 to 10 minutes. Shape into a ball. Place in a lightly oiled bowl. Turn once to oil all surfaces. Cover the bowl with a damp dish towel. Let rise in a warm place until doubled in bulk. This should take about 1 hour. Punch dough down. Turn out onto a lightly floured surface. Divide into two portions. Shape each into a ball. Cover with the towel and let dough rest for 10 minutes.

Grease two 9x5x3-inch loaf pans. Shape each portion of dough into a loaf. This can be done by simply pulling the dough into a loaf shape and tucking the edges under. Place the loaves into the prepared pans. Cover with the damp towel. Let rise in a warm place until the dough rises above the top of the pan. This should take 40 to 50 minutes.

(continued)

Preheat the oven to 375 degrees F. (350 degrees F. if you use a glass loaf dish). Bake for about 45 minutes. If the top browns too quickly, cover it loosely with a piece of foil for the last 15 to 20 minutes of baking. Tap the loaf on top. If it sounds hollow, it's done. Remove from the pan immediately. Cool on a rack. When completely cooled, cover with plastic wrap or place in a lock-type plastic bag.

BASIC SWEET ROLL DOUGH

Yield: enough for two 9-inch coffeecakes or about 24 sweet rolls

This is what I refer to as my "super" dough. It can quickly be turned into all kinds of sweet rolls and coffeecakes, recipes for some of which follow. It's simple to make and easy to use.

1 teaspoon plus ¼ cup sugar
¼ cup warm water
1 (¼ oz.) package active dry yeast
1 cup milk
1 egg
½ teaspoon salt
4 tablespoons butter or margarine, melted
3½ to 4½ cups all-purpose flour

Combine the 1 teaspoon sugar, warm water, and yeast. Stir to mix. Set aside until bubbly.

In a large mixing bowl, combine the ¼ cup sugar, milk, egg, salt, and butter. Mix well. Add 1 cup of the flour and the yeast mixture. Mix well. Gradually add enough of the remaining flour to make a moderately firm dough.

On a lightly floured surface, knead the dough until it is smooth. This will probably take 4 to 5 minutes. Shape the dough into a ball. Place into a large oiled bowl. Turn the dough so that all surfaces are lightly oiled. Cover and allow to rise in a warm place for about 1 hour, or until the dough has doubled in bulk. Punch down and divide in half. Cover each portion with a dry dish towel and let it rest for about 10 minutes. Use for coffeecakes or sweet rolls.

CINNAMON RUM ROLLS

Yield: 24 rolls

*T*he soaked raisins give these cinnamon rolls a faint taste of rum. Heavy cream poured over the rolls before they are baked makes them creamy soft.

1 cup raisins
⅔ cup light rum
Basic Sweet Roll Dough (page 232)
4 tablespoons butter or margarine, melted
½ cup sugar
2 teaspoons ground cinnamon
½ cup chopped pecans
⅔ cup heavy cream

GLAZE
2 to 2½ cups confectioners' sugar
4 to 5 tablespoons milk

Combine the raisins and rum in a small bowl. Allow to sit for at least 1 hour. You might want to soak the raisins overnight in the refrigerator.

Grease two 9-inch cake pans. After the dough has risen the first time and has been punched down, divide the dough in half. Roll each portion to a rectangle about 9x12 inches. Brush each rectangle with melted butter.

In a small bowl, combine the sugar, cinnamon, and pecans. Stir to mix. Sprinkle this mixture over the buttered dough. Drain the raisins and sprinkle over the sugar mixture. Roll the dough jelly-roll fashion, starting with the 12-inch side. Cut into slices ¾ to 1 inch thick. Place the slices cut side down

(continued)

in the cake pans. Cover and allow to rise in a warm place for about 45 minutes, or until doubled.

Preheat the oven to 375 degrees F. Pour ⅓ cup of the cream over each pan of rolls. Bake for 18 to 20 minutes. Remove from the oven and turn the rolls out onto a plate. Invert onto another plate so that rolls will be upright. Cool slightly.

For the glaze, combine the confectioners' sugar and milk in a small bowl. Beat until smooth. Drizzle over cinnamon rolls.

PINEAPPLE CREAM ROLLS

Yield: 24 sweet rolls

A pineapple, cream cheese, and walnut filling gives these soft rolls a crunchy, sweet swirl. If you have a pineapple lover in your family, these are sure to hit the spot. If you like spices, try adding a little ground cinnamon and ground ginger to the filling. Don't add much because you don't want to mask the delicious pineapple flavor.

Basic Sweet Roll Dough (page 232)
6 ounces cream cheese, softened at room temperature
½ cup pineapple preserves
¾ cup chopped walnuts

PINEAPPLE ICING

2 cups confectioners' sugar
4 tablespoons pineapple preserves
3 to 4 tablespoons milk

After the basic dough has risen the first time and has been punched down, divide it into two portions. Shape each of these portions into a ball, cover with a towel, and let the dough rest for about 10 minutes.

While the dough is resting, combine the cream cheese and pineapple preserves in a small mixing bowl. Beat until smooth. Grease two 9-inch round cake pans.

Roll each portion of dough on a lightly floured surface to a 9x12-inch rectangle. Spread each rectangle with half the cream cheese mixture. Sprinkle with walnuts. Roll up from the 12-inch side. Pinch the edges together to seal. Cut into slices about 1 inch thick. Place rolls cut side down in pans. Cover with the towel and allow to rise in a warm place until almost doubled, or 30 to 45 minutes.

Preheat the oven to 375 degrees F.

Bake the rolls for 18 to 20 minutes, or until lightly browned. Turn out of pan onto a plate. Invert onto another plate so that rolls will be right side up. Cool slightly.

To make the icing, combine all the icing ingredients in a small bowl. Beat until smooth. Spread over rolls.

OATMEAL COOKIE SWIRLS

Yield: 24 swirls

The flavor possibilities with these swirls are limitless. You can have chocolate swirls by substituting chocolate wafer crumbs for the oatmeal cookie crumbs, or coconut macaroon swirls by using coconut cookie crumbs. Another way of changing the rolls is to dip them in melted butterscotch, peanut butter, chocolate, or mint chips and then roll them in cookie crumbs. If you use the chips, you will need to add 1 to 2 tablespoons of shortening with each cup of chips when melting. Don't use butter or margarine.

Basic Sweet Roll Dough (page 232)
5½ tablespoons butter or margarine, melted
1¾ cups fine oatmeal cookie crumbs

VANILLA GLAZE
2 cups confectioners' sugar
3 to 4 tablespoons milk
¼ teaspoon vanilla extract

Grease two 12-cup muffin tins. After the basic dough has risen the first time and has been punched down., divide it into two portions. Divide each of these portions into 12 smaller portions. Roll each small portion of dough between the palms of the hands until you get a rope about 9 inches long. Dip the rope in the melted butter and then roll it in the cookie crumbs. Swirl the rope in a muffin cup, pushing the end into the center of the swirl. Repeat with remaining dough. Cover each pan of rolls with a towel and let rise until almost doubled, or 30 to 40 minutes.

Preheat the oven to 375 degrees F. Bake for 18 to 20 minutes. Remove from muffin tins immediately and cool on a rack.

Combine all glaze ingredients in a small bowl. Beat until smooth. Drizzle over warm swirls.

HERB POTATO ROLLS

Yield: 24 cloverleaf rolls

*T*he flavor combination of ranch-style dressing mix and buttermilk gives these potato rolls a unique and delightful flavor.

¼ cup warm water
3 tablespoons sugar
2 packages (¼ oz. each) active dry yeast
1 cup buttermilk
1 cup cooked mashed potatoes
7 tablespoons butter or margarine, melted
1 package (¼ oz.) ranch-style dressing mix
1 egg
4 to 4½ cups bread flour

Combine the warm water, 1 tablespoon of the sugar, and the yeast in a small bowl. Stir to mix. Set aside until bubbly.

In a large bowl, combine the buttermilk, potatoes, 4 tablespoons of the melted butter, dressing mix, remaining 2 tablespoons sugar, and egg. Stir until well mixed. Add 1 cup of the flour and the yeast mixture. Mix well. Continue adding flour about 1 cup at a time until dough is stiff enough to knead. Turn out onto a lightly floured surface. Knead until smooth and elastic. This will take 4 to 5 minutes. Put dough into an oiled bowl. Turn the dough so that all surfaces will be lightly oiled. Cover the bowl with a dish towel and put in a warm place until the dough has doubled in size. This usually takes about 1 hour.

Grease two (12 sections each) muffin tins. Punch the dough down and turn out onto a lightly floured surface. Be sure all air bubbles are punched out. Pinch off small portions of the dough and roll each between the palms of your hands to make smooth balls about 1 inch in diameter. Pinch tops of 3 small balls together to make a cloverleaf roll and put the roll, pinched side down, in a muffin cup. Repeat with remaining dough. Cover the pans with dish towels. Put in a warm place until dough has doubled in size, 30 to 40 minutes.

Preheat the oven to 400 degrees F.

(continued)

Brush the rolls with 1½ tablespoons of the melted butter. Bake the rolls for 8 to 10 minutes, or until lightly browned and no longer doughy. As soon as the rolls come from the oven, brush with remaining 1½ tablespoons melted butter. Serve warm.

STRAWBERRY TWIST COFFEECAKE

Yield: 16 servings

Easy and beautiful! This yeast dough is very pliable and can be stretched without breaking. Homemade jam or preserves adds a much better flavor than the commercial kind. You can vary the kinds of jam and have a new flavor treat each time. You can also use different kinds of cookie crumbs.

1 teaspoon plus ¼ cup sugar
¼ cup warm water
1 (¼ oz.) package active dry yeast
1 egg
¼ cup vegetable oil
1 cup milk
1 teaspoon salt
3 to 4 cups all-purpose flour
½ cup chopped pecans
⅔ cup finely crushed crisp coconut cookies
4 tablespoons butter, melted
1 cup strawberry jam or preserves

GLAZE
1½ cups confectioners' sugar
2 to 3 tablespoons milk
¼ teaspoon vanilla extract

Combine the 1 teaspoon sugar, warm water, and yeast in a small bowl. Stir to mix. Set aside until bubbly.

In a large bowl, combine the remaining ¼ cup sugar, egg, oil, milk, and salt. Stir to mix. Add 1 cup of the flour and mix. Stir in the yeast mixture. Add enough of the remaining flour to make a soft dough. Knead the dough on a lightly floured surface until smooth. Place in an oiled bowl. Turn so that all the dough is coated with the oil. Cover and let rise in a warm place until light and doubled in bulk. This should take about 1 hour.

While the dough is rising, prepare the nut filling. In a small bowl, combine the chopped pecans and the crushed cookies.

After the dough has risen, punch it down and divide it into 3 equal pieces. On a lightly floured surface, roll one portion of the dough to a 12-inch circle. Don't worry if the circle is not exact because this dough can be pulled to correct size. Place the first circle onto a 12-inch pizza pan. Brush with 2 table-spoons of the melted butter. Sprinkle with half the cookie mixture. Continue with the next portion of dough. After it is rolled, place it on top of the first circle. Spread the jam over the dough. Roll the third portion into a 12-inch circle and place on top of the jam-covered circle. Brush with remaining 2 tablespoons of butter and sprinkle with remaining cookie mixture.

Place a glass (about 2 inches in diameter) upside down in the center of the circle. Do not press it into the dough. The glass is used only to mark the center. Cut the dough into 16 wedges, cutting just to the glass. Twist each three-layered section five times, and lay back on the pan. Remove the glass. Cover and allow to rise until doubled. This should take 40 to 45 minutes.

Preheat the oven to 375 degrees F. Bake for 20 to 25 minutes, until golden brown and no longer doughy. Cool slightly.

To make the glaze, combine the confectioners' sugar, milk, and vanilla extract in a small bowl. Beat until smooth. Drizzle over coffeecake.

BAKER'S ORANGE TWISTS

Yield: 20 twists

*T*hese sweet rolls were developed on the same day that Billy Baker, a young man in our neighborhood, was making his first appearance in the political arena. As I glanced out my kitchen window, I saw friends gathering at his home to join in the victory celebration. I sent my congratulations in the form of a baker's dozen of orange twists. I will never forget his note of thanks in which he stated that these were the hit of the party and had made his victory even "sweeter."

1 teaspoon plus ⅔ cup sugar
¼ cup warm water
1 (¼ oz.) package active dry yeast
1 cup freshly squeezed orange juice
½ teaspoon salt
1 egg
4 tablespoons butter or margarine, melted
4½ to 5 cups all-purpose flour
½ cup orange marmalade
½ teaspoon ground cinnamon
⅔ cup finely chopped pecans

ORANGE GLAZE
2 cups confectioners' sugar
4 to 5 tablespoons orange juice

Combine the 1 teaspoon sugar with the warm water. Sprinkle the yeast over the top. Stir to mix. Set aside until the mixture becomes bubbly.

In a large bowl, combine the orange juice, ⅓ cup of the sugar, salt, egg, and butter. Stir in 1 cup of the flour and the yeast mixture. Gradually add the remaining flour until you get a moderately firm dough. Turn the dough out onto a lightly floured surface. Knead 3 to 4 minutes, until smooth and elastic. Form the dough into a ball. Place in an oiled bowl. Turn the dough so that all surfaces are oiled. Cover the bowl with a dish towel. Allow to rise in a warm place until doubled in bulk. This should take about 1 hour. Punch down and divide the dough into two portions. Roll each portion of dough to a 10x15-inch rectangle. Spread each rectangle with a thin layer of marmalade.

Combine the remaining ⅓ cup sugar with the cinnamon and pecans in a small bowl. Mix well. Sprinkle this mixture over rectangles. Cut each rectangle into strips, 15x1 inch each. (I like to use a pizza cutter for these strips.) Fold the strips in half, enclosing the marmalade in the middle, reducing the strips to 7½x1 inch each. Twist each strip 5 or 6 times.

Lightly grease 2 cookie sheets or line 2 jelly-roll pans (10x15x1 inch each) with aluminum foil. Place the orange twists on the baking sheets, leaving about 1 inch between each twist. Cover with a dish towel. Allow to rise until light and almost doubled. This will take about 45 minutes.

Preheat the oven to 375 degrees F. Bake the twists for 12 to 15 minutes, until lightly browned. Remove from the baking sheets and place on a rack to cool.

For the glaze, combine the confectioners' sugar and orange juice in a small bowl. Beat until smooth. Drizzle over slightly warm orange twists.

CHOCOLATE CARAMEL
STICKY ROLLS

....

Yield: 24 sticky rolls

One word comes to mind when I enjoy one of these sticky rolls: "turtle." I am not exactly sure when the combination of chocolate, caramel, and pecans was first referred to as "turtles" but I do remember a popular caramel and pecan candy coated with chocolate with "legs" and "head" made from pecan pieces. This made the candy resemble a turtle and I suppose the name caught on. Now just about everything that has this flavor combo seems to be called "turtle." We have turtle cheesecake, turtle cookies, turtle brownies, and turtle cake. These newly developed rolls fit the image also. The chocolate-flavored yeast dough is spread with a cream cheese and brown sugar filling that adds a slight taste of caramel. The rolls are baked on top of a mixture of pecans and caramel ice cream topping. Scrumptious!

1 teaspoon plus ⅓ cup sugar
¼ cup warm water
1 (¼ oz.) package dry yeast
⅔ cup heavy cream
1 egg
½ teaspoon salt
¼ cup cocoa
3 to 3½ cups all-purpose flour
1 (12 oz.) jar caramel ice cream topping
1 cup coarsely chopped pecans
8 ounces cream cheese, softened at room temperature
½ cup firmly packed light brown sugar
1 cup finely chopped pecans

In a small bowl, combine the 1 teaspoon sugar with the warm water and yeast. Stir and set aside until the mixture becomes bubbly.

In a large mixing bowl, combine the ⅓ cup sugar, cream, egg, and salt. Stir until mixed. Add the yeast mixture, cocoa, and 2 cups of the flour. Mix well. Gradually add enough of the remaining flour to make a moderately firm dough. On a lightly floured surface, knead the dough about 5 minutes, or until smooth. Shape the dough into a ball and place it into a large oiled bowl. Turn the dough to coat all surfaces with the oil. Cover and allow to rise in a warm place for about 1 hour, or until doubled in bulk.

Grease a 9x13x2-inch baking pan. Pour the caramel ice cream topping into the pan and spread evenly. Sprinkle with the coarsely chopped pecans.

In a medium bowl, combine the cream cheese and brown sugar. Mix well.

After the dough has risen the first time, punch it down. On a lightly floured surface, roll the dough to a 12x18-inch rectangle. Spread the cream cheese mixture over the dough and sprinkle with the finely chopped pecans. Roll jelly-roll fashion, starting with the 18-inch side. Cut into slices about ¾ inch thick. Place cut side down on top of the caramel mixture in the baking pan.

Cover the pans with a dish towel and allow the rolls to rise in a warm place for about 45 minutes, or until almost doubled.

Preheat the oven to 375 degrees F. Bake for 18 to 20 minutes. Remove from the oven and turn out onto a large serving platter.

New Breads on the Rise

SOUTHERN YEAST
BISCUIT DOUGH

Yield: about 8 cups of dough, yielding about 30 biscuits or rolls

The "rising" star in the biscuit family is the yeast biscuit. This versatile yeast dough doesn't need to rise before baking because it is made with self-rising flour and baking soda, but gives the yeast flavor Southerners love so much. With this easy-to-make yeast dough in the refrigerator, no one should be without biscuits for breakfast. This is also excellent for making quick sweet rolls and coffeecakes.

¼ cup warm water
2 tablespoons sugar
2 packages (¼ oz. each) active dry yeast
5 cups self-rising flour
1 teaspoon baking soda
1 cup shortening
2 cups buttermilk

Combine the water and sugar in a small bowl. Stir in the yeast. Set aside until the mixture becomes bubbly.

In a large mixing bowl, combine the flour and baking soda. Stir to mix. Cut in the shortening using a pastry blender, a fork, or your fingertips until the mixture resembles cornmeal. Add the yeast mixture and buttermilk. Stir with a large wooden spoon until well mixed. This will not be a smooth dough. Cover the bowl with plastic wrap and refrigerate the dough until needed; it will keep about 1 week.

YEAST BISCUITS

Yield: 6 biscuits

1½ cups Southern Yeast Biscuit Dough (page 246)

Preheat the oven to 450 degrees F. Grease a baking sheet.

On a lightly floured surface, knead the dough gently 2 or 3 times. Pat or roll to about a ½-inch thickness. Cut with a 2-inch biscuit cutter. Place on baking sheet, spacing the biscuits about 1 inch apart. Bake for 7 to 8 minutes, until lightly browned.

HERB BUBBLE LOAF

Yield: about 6 servings

A great bread to enjoy with a dish of spaghetti. It is also wonderful just eaten while hot with a little extra butter. It does not have to rise before baking because it is made with the special Southern yeast biscuit dough.

5½ tablespoons butter or margarine, melted
1 garlic clove, minced (about ½ teaspoon)
½ teaspoon dried parsley
¼ teaspoon dried dill weed
4 cups Southern Yeast Biscuit Dough (page 246)
¼ teaspoon poppy seeds
1 teaspoon sesame seeds

Preheat the oven to 375 degrees F.

In a small bowl, combine the butter, garlic, parsley, and dill weed. Spoon the dough onto a floured surface. Knead about 6 times. Pinch off portions about the size of golf balls. Dip the dough balls into the herb butter, coating well. Place the balls in a 9x5x3-inch loaf pan, making 2 layers if necessary. Sprinkle the poppy seeds and sesame seeds on top. Bake for about 40 minutes, until golden brown. Remove from the pan immediately. Best served warm.

EASY CINNAMON ROLLS

Yield: about 8 servings

*T*hese rolls are easy because they are made from the "no-rise" yeast biscuit dough. The texture is not quite as light and fluffy as standard yeast cinnamon rolls, but the ease of preparation compensates for the slight difference.

3 cups Southern Yeast Biscuit Dough (page 246)
4 tablespoons butter or margarine, melted
⅓ cup sugar
1 teaspoon ground cinnamon
½ cup raisins

CONFECTIONERS' SUGAR GLAZE

1 cup confectioners' sugar
1 to 1½ tablespoons milk
¼ teaspoon vanilla extract

Preheat the oven to 375 degrees F. Butter a 9-inch cake pan.

Gently knead the dough 2 or 3 times on a lightly floured surface. Work as little flour into the dough as possible. Roll to an 8x18-inch rectangle. Brush with the melted butter.

In a small bowl, combine the sugar, cinnamon, and raisins. Mix well. Sprinkle over the dough. Roll jelly-roll fashion, starting with the 18-inch side. Cut into about 16 slices. Place in the prepared pan. Bake for 18 to 20 minutes, until light brown. Turn out of the pan onto a rack and then turn upright onto serving dish.

For the glaze, combine the confectioners' sugar, milk, and vanilla in a small bowl. Beat until smooth. Drizzle over cinnamon rolls. Best served slightly warm.

CINNAMON TOAST STICKS

Yield: about 20 sticks, serving 10

These crispy cinnamon sticks served with a cup of coffee make a perfect "eat and run" breakfast. Quick and easy to make because they are made from refrigerated yeast biscuit dough. If you want only one, pinch off a small portion of dough, form it into a stick, dip it in butter, and roll in a mixture of cinnamon and sugar.

3 cups Southern Yeast Biscuit Dough (page 246)
1 cup sugar
1 teaspoon ground cinnamon
¼ pound (1 stick) butter, melted

Preheat the oven to 375 degrees F.

Spoon the dough onto a well-floured surface. Knead in enough flour to make a moderately firm dough. Pinch off portions about the size of a large walnut. Roll between the palms of your hands to get a rope 6 to 7 inches long. If you want thinner sticks, use portions about the size of large marbles.

Combine the sugar and cinnamon. Pour onto a piece of wax paper or aluminum foil. Dip the rope into melted butter. Roll in sugar mixture to coat. Give each rope a few twists. Place on an ungreased baking sheet. Bake for about 20 minutes, until crisp and lightly browned. If you are making the thinner toast sticks, check them after 10 minutes of baking. Remove from the baking sheet immediately. Cool on a rack.

APPLE BUTTER ROLLS

Yield: 16 rolls

*T*hese were made especially for Mauna, my number one assistant in the test kitchen. She loves apple butter with just about everything and was thrilled when I told her we were going to test a new yeast bread recipe with an apple butter filling. After tasting one of the rolls, she quickly gave them the thumbs up.

3 cups Southern Yeast Biscuit Dough (page 246)
4 ounces cream cheese, softened at room temperature
⅓ cup apple butter
½ cup firmly packed light brown sugar
1½ cups confectioners' sugar
2½ tablespoons apple juice

Preheat the oven to 375 degrees F. Butter a 9-inch cake pan. Spoon the soft dough onto a well-floured surface. Knead until smooth. Roll to a rectangle about 10x16 inches.

In a medium bowl, combine the cream cheese, apple butter, and brown sugar. Beat until smooth. Spread over dough. Roll jelly-roll fashion, starting with the 16-inch side. Cut into 1-inch slices. Place slices cut side down in cake pan. Bake for about 20 minutes, or until rolls are lightly browned and no longer doughy. Turn out onto a plate and then invert onto another plate so that rolls will be right side up.

Combine the confectioners' sugar and apple juice in a small bowl. Beat until smooth. Drizzle over rolls.

Busy Baker Breads

QUICK BREADS

YEAST BREADS

Quick Breads

••••••••••)》◈《(•••••••••

EASY CHEESY BISCUITS

Yield: about 10 biscuits

This is just another tasty version of the famous whipping cream biscuits.

2 cups self-rising flour
1 cup heavy cream (not whipped)
½ cup grated Cheddar cheese
Melted butter for coating biscuits

Preheat the oven to 400 degrees F.

In a medium bowl or in the bowl of a food processor, combine the flour, cream, and cheese. Mix until the mixture forms a ball. Roll out on a lightly floured surface to a thickness of about ½ inch. Cut with a 1½- or 2-inch biscuit cutter. Dip each biscuit in the melted butter. Place on an ungreased cookie sheet, spacing the biscuits about 1 inch apart. Bake for 10 to 15 minutes, until lightly browned.

GARLIC BUTTER BISCUITS

Yield: about 8 biscuits

*T*errific! That's the best one-word description I can think of for these buttery jewels. When you serve these, no one will ever believe that they could be so easy to make. They are crisp with butter and garlic on the outside, yet light and fluffy on the inside. If you like cheese, add about ½ cup finely shredded Cheddar cheese to the batter.

4 tablespoons butter or margarine
1 teaspoon finely minced garlic
1 teaspoon finely minced fresh parsley
1½ cups buttermilk baking mix
½ cup milk

Preheat the oven to 400 degrees F. Melt the butter in a small saucepan. Add the garlic and cook over medium heat for about 30 seconds, stirring constantly. Add the parsley and cook for another 10 seconds. Set aside.

Combine the buttermilk baking mix with the milk in a medium bowl. Beat until blended. This mixture will be thick. Pinch off portions and roll in the palms of your hands to about the size of golf balls. Flatten slightly. Dip each biscuit in the butter mixture and place on a baking sheet, spacing them about 1 inch apart. Bake for 10 minutes. Remove from oven and brush the tops with the remaining butter mixture. Return to oven and bake an additional 4 to 5 minutes, until golden brown. Serve warm.

HINT-OF-MINT
CRESCENT SWIRLS

....

Yield: 12 crescent swirls

*T*hese are good to make after the holidays when there is a surplus of pepper-mint candy canes. The use of refrigerated crescent roll dough helps the hurried baker prepare sweet treats for the family.

1 can (8 count) refrigerated crescent roll dough
3 ounces cream cheese
½ cup confectioners' sugar
⅓ cup finely crushed peppermint candy canes

GLAZE
1 cup confectioners' sugar
1½ to 2 tablespoons milk or water

Preheat the oven to 375 degrees F. Line a cookie sheet with aluminum foil.

Unroll the crescent dough sections. Do not separate them into crescents. Place the two rectangular sections together, overlapping edges, to make an 8x12-inch rectangle. Press the edges and perforations to seal well.

Combine the cream cheese and confectioners' sugar in a medium bowl. Beat until smooth. Spread over the dough. Sprinkle surface with crushed pep-permint candy. Roll jelly-roll fashion from the 12-inch side. Cut into 1-inch slices. Place on cookie sheet, cut side down. Flatten slightly with the fingertips. Bake for 18 to 20 minutes, until lightly browned. Remove from the cookie sheet and place on a rack to cool.

To make the glaze, combine the sugar and milk in a small bowl. Beat until smooth. Drizzle over swirls.

BLUE-BERRIED TREASURES

Yield: 10 sweet rolls

$\mathcal{T}$he use of canned biscuits makes these sweet rolls quick and easy.

2 cans (10 count each) refrigerated buttermilk biscuits
3 tablespoons butter or margarine, melted
1 cup finely crushed coconut cookie crumbs (crisp cookies, not soft
* macaroons)*
10 teaspoons blueberry preserves
1 cup confectioners' sugar
1½ tablespoons lemon juice

Preheat the oven to 400 degrees F. Lightly grease a cookie sheet.

Roll 2 biscuits at a time together between the palms of your hands to form a rope about 10 inches long. Dip the rope into the melted butter. Roll in cookie crumbs to coat. If the rope shrinks during coating, give it a gentle pull back to 10 inches. Swirl into a coil, pinching ends together to seal. Place on cookie sheet. Press your thumb or a spoon into the middle of the coil to make a large thumbprint. Spoon 1 teaspoon of the preserves into the indention. Bake for 10 to 12 minutes, until lightly browned.

While the sweet rolls are baking, mix together the confectioners' sugar and lemon juice. Beat until smooth. Allow the rolls to cool slightly on a rack before drizzling the lemon glaze over each roll.

PLUM POCKETS

....

Yield: 10 small breakfast turnovers

*I*nside each little breakfast "turnover" is a surprise pocket of plum jam. The use of canned biscuits makes preparation a snap.

1 (10 count) can refrigerated flaky buttermilk biscuits
15 teaspoons plum jam
2 cups confectioners' sugar
4 to 5 tablespoons milk

Preheat the oven to 400 degrees F. Line a baking sheet with aluminum foil.

Press each biscuit to a thin circle 3½ to 4 inches in diameter. Put 1½ teaspoons plum jam in the center of each biscuit circle. Fold over, making a miniature turnover. Pinch the edges to seal well to prevent the jam from seeping out during baking. Place turnovers on the cookie sheet, spacing them about 2 inches apart. Bake for 8 to 10 minutes, until golden brown.

While the turnovers are baking, combine the confectioners' sugar and milk in a small bowl. Beat until smooth. This should be a pourable mixture that is a little thinner than a drizzle glaze. As soon as the turnovers come from the oven, dip them into the glaze mixture, coating well. Place on a rack for the glaze to set.

AMBROSIA ENGLISH MUFFINS

Yield: 6 servings

*T*he orange filling seeps into the porous texture of the English muffin, and the coconut stays on top forming a puffy macaroon layer. This is a quick-and-easy treat that can fit into a busy schedule.

1 egg
2 tablespoons butter or margarine, melted
½ cup sugar
⅛ teaspoon salt
½ teaspoon vanilla extract
1 tablespoon freshly squeezed orange juice
½ cup fine coconut (see note)
3 English muffins, split

Preheat the oven to 375 degrees F.

In a small bowl, beat the egg until light and pale yellow. Add the butter, sugar, salt, vanilla, and orange juice. Mix until well blended. Stir in the coconut. Spoon about 2 tablespoons of the ambrosia on top of each muffin half, spreading it to cover the top. Place the halves on an ungreased cookie sheet. Bake for 20 to 25 minutes, or until the topping puffs and turns golden brown. Best served warm.

NOTE: Unsweetened macaroon coconut is best, but if it is not available, you can process canned coconut in a food processor until it is fine-textured but not powdery. You can also use the coconut as is and the muffins are still great!

MELTAWAY
BLUEBERRY COFFEECAKE

Yield: about 12 servings

*T*his quick coffeecake is so moist that it melts in your mouth. The blueberry-pecan ribbon through the center of the coffeecake adds a special flavorful touch. There is just a hint of cinnamon. You don't want the spice to overpower the blueberries.

2 cups fresh blueberries (or quick-frozen blueberries without sugar added)
1½ cups sugar
½ cup chopped pecans
½ pound (2 sticks) butter or margarine, softened at room temperature
1 teaspoon vanilla extract
2 eggs
2½ cups self-rising flour
⅛ teaspoon ground cinnamon
1 cup sour cream

GLAZE
1 cup confectioners' sugar
1½ to 2 tablespoons milk or water
¼ teaspoon vanilla extract

Preheat the oven to 350 degrees F. Grease and lightly flour a 9x13x2-inch baking pan.

In a medium bowl, combine the blueberries, ¼ cup of the sugar, and pecans. Mix well and set aside.

In a large mixing bowl, cream together the remaining 1¼ cups sugar with the butter and vanilla. Add the eggs one at a time, beating well after each addition. Add the flour, cinnamon, and sour cream. Mix well. Spread about 2 cups of the batter in the prepared pan. Spoon the blueberry mixture over the batter. Drop the remaining batter from a tablespoon over the filling. The blueberry filling does not need to be completely covered with batter. A few blueberries peeking through make the coffeecake more attractive. Bake for 40 to 45 minutes, or until a wooden pick comes out clean when inserted near the center of the coffeecake. Allow to cool slightly on a wire rack.

To make the glaze, combine all glaze ingredients and beat until smooth. Drizzle over cooled coffeecake.

SPEEDY CINNAMON BUNS

Yield: about 12 buns

*N*o cinnamon bun could be easier to make. But ease of preparation is not all these delicious sweet rolls have to offer. They taste great!

2 cups buttermilk baking mix
½ cup firmly packed light brown sugar
1¼ teaspoons ground cinnamon
½ cup milk
½ cup raisins

GLAZE
1½ cups confectioners' sugar
¼ teaspoon vanilla extract
2 to 3 tablespoons milk

Preheat the oven to 400 degrees F. Grease a cookie sheet.

Combine the baking mix, brown sugar, and cinnamon in a large bowl. Stir to mix. Add the milk. Beat until well blended. Stir in the raisins. This mixture will be thick. Using about ¼ cup per bun, drop batter onto the cookie sheet, spacing the buns about 2 inches apart. Flatten slightly with the back of a spoon. Bake for 12 to 15 minutes, until lightly browned. Place on a rack and cool about 3 minutes.

Combine the glaze ingredients. Beat until smooth. Drizzle over warm cinnamon buns.

Yeast Breads

---•◦◦●◦●◦◦•---

YEAST MUFFINS

....

Yield: 24 yeast muffins

*W*hen you want the old-fashioned, double-rise yeast rolls but don't have the time to make them, try this quick-and-easy version of yeast muffins. This soft dough will keep well in the refrigerator for a week.

2 cups warm water
2 tablespoons sugar
1 (¼ oz.) package active dry yeast
11 tablespoons butter or margarine, melted
1 egg, slightly beaten
4 cups self-rising flour

Preheat the oven to 400 degrees F. Grease two 12-cup muffin tins (⅓ cup capacity each).

Combine the water and sugar in a large bowl. Sprinkle the yeast over the top and stir in. Add butter and egg. Mix well. Gradually add the flour, mixing well. Spoon into greased muffin tins, filling about half full. Bake for about 15 minutes, until lightly browned and no longer doughy. Serve warm with butter.

EASY MARMALADE COFFEECAKE

Yield: 12 to 15 servings

*T*his quick breakfast treat gives you the delicious flavor of a yeast bread with the ease of a quick batter bread. There is no kneading and the bread doesn't have to rise before baking. The texture is cakelike but the flavor is definitely coffeecake.

1 teaspoon plus ¾ cup sugar
¼ cup warm water
1 (¼ oz.) package active dry yeast
1 cup buttermilk, at room temperature
1 egg
3 cups self-rising flour
12 tablespoons (1½ sticks) butter or margarine, melted
½ cup orange marmalade
½ cup firmly packed light brown sugar
½ cup chopped walnuts

Preheat the oven to 350 degrees F.

Mix together the 1 teaspoon sugar, warm water, and yeast in a small bowl. Set aside until bubbly. Combine the buttermilk, egg, remaining ¾ cup sugar, flour, ½ cup of the melted butter, and yeast mixture. Mix well.

Pour the remaining ¼ cup melted butter into a 9x13x2-inch baking pan. Stir in the marmalade and spread in bottom of pan. Combine the brown sugar and walnuts. Sprinkle over the marmalade mixture. Pour batter into pan and smooth the top. Bake for 35 minutes, until lightly browned and no longer doughy. Invert onto a serving dish. If any of the marmalade topping sticks to the pan, simply scrape it off and spread it over the warm coffeecake.

Index